W9-APH-894

THE AFRICAN AND MIDDLE EASTERN WORLD, 600–1500

BONNIE G. SMITH
GENERAL EDITOR

THE AFRICAN AND MIDDLE EASTERN WORLD, 600–1500

Randall L. Pouwels

OXFORD
UNIVERSITY PRESS

For Joel, Eric, Ethan, Ellie, and Lauren

OXFORD
UNIVERSITY PRESS

Oxford University Press, Inc., publishes works that further Oxford University's objective of excellence in research, scholarship, and education.

Oxford New York
Auckland   Cape Town   Dar es Salaam   Hong Kong   Karachi
Kuala Lumpur   Madrid   Melbourne   Mexico City   Nairobi
New Delhi   Shanghai   Taipei   Toronto

With offices in
Argentina   Austria   Brazil   Chile   Czech Republic   France   Greece
Guatemala   Hungary   Italy   Japan   Poland   Portugal   Singapore
South Korea   Switzerland   Thailand   Turkey   Ukraine   Vietnam

Copyright © 2005 by Oxford University Press, Inc.

Published by Oxford University Press, Inc.
198 Madison Avenue, New York, New York 10016
www.oup.com

Oxford is a registered trademark of Oxford University Press

Design: Stephanie Blumenthal and Alexis Siroc
Layout: Mary Neal Meador
Cover design and logo: Nora Wertz

Library of Congress Cataloging-in-Publication Data
Pouwels, Randall Lee
African and Middle Eastern world, 600-1500 / Randall L. Pouwels.
p. cm. — (Medieval & early modern world)
ISBN-13: 978-019-517673-5 — 978-019-522265-4 (Calif. ed.) — 978-019-522157-2 (set)
ISBN-10: 0-19-517673-1 — 0-19-522265-2 (California ed.) — 0-19-522157-5 (set)
1. Civilization, Islamic. 2. Middle East. 3. Africa. I. Title. II. Medieval and early modern world.
DS36.85.P68 2005
956'.01—dc22
2004021476

9 8 7 6 5 4 3 2 1

Printed in the United States of America on acid-free paper

On the cover: A standing warrior in bronze, from the lower Niger River valley.
Frontispiece: A man plays a pipe and another the tambourine in this 16th-century Persian painting of a picnic.

BONNIE G. SMITH
GENERAL EDITOR

DIANE L. BROOKS, Ed.D.
EDUCATION CONSULTANT

CONTENTS

A 66 marks a primary source—a piece of writing that speaks to us from the past.

CAST OF CHARACTERS

Every Arab has at least three names: a personal (or "first") name; the name of his or her father; and the name of his or her father's clan. For example, the prophet Muhammad's father's name was Abdallah and his clan was the Hashimite clan, so Muhammad's full name was Muhammad ibn Abdallah al-Hashimi. This means Muhammad, son of Abdallah the Hashimite. Ibn (or bin) means "son of," and al-means "the."

Abdallah (ub-duh-LAH) **ibn Yasin** (yah-SEEN), died 1059 • Moroccan Islamic scholar who led, until his death, a holy war called the Almoravid jihad

Abu (uh-BOO) **Bakr** (BACK-er), around 573–634 • Muhammad's closest friend and the first male to convert to Islam; became first caliph in 632

Abu (uh-BOO) **Bakr** (BACK-er) **Muhammad** (moo-HAH-mud) **ar-Razi** (ar-RAH-zee), around 865–935 • Persian physician

Abu (uh-BOO) **Talib** (TAH-lib), died 619 • Muhammad's uncle, who raised Muhammad when he became an orphan

Ahmad (AH-muhd) **ibn Hanbal** (HAHN-bahl), 780–855 • Founder of one of the most important, and the most conservative, schools of Islamic law

Alhazen (al-huh-ZEHN), 965–1039 • Arab physicist and mathematician

Ali (AH-lee), around 600–661 • Fourth caliph, assassinated by a Kharijite fanatic

Askia (as-KEE-yuh) **Muhammad** (moo-HAH-mud) **Turé** (too-RAY), died1528 • Songhay emperor from 1493 to 1528 and founder of Askia dynasty

Al-Biruni (AL-bee-ROO-nee), 974–1048 • Arab scholar of history, geography, medicine, chemistry, mathematics, and astronomy

Ewuare (ewe-WAH-ray) **the Great**, 15th century • General and statesman who increased the power of the Kingdom of Benin

Fatima (FA-tuh-muh), around 606–32 • Daughter of Muhammad and wife of Ali

Al-Ghazali (al-guh-ZA-lee), 1058–1111 • Most respected religious scholar of his time; made Sufism, or Islamic mysticism, acceptable to orthodox scholars

Harun (huh-ROON) **al-Rashid** (al-ruh-SHEED), 763–809 • Fifth Abbasid caliph, who made Baghdad a very prosperous city

Hasan (hah-SAHN) **bin Sulayman** (soo-lay-MAHN), 14th century • King of Kilwa

Ibn Battuta (buh-TOO-tuh), born 1304 • Berber from Tangier, Morocco, who left an account of his 75,000-mile journey throughout the Islamic world

Ibn Rushd (ROOSHT), 1126–98 • Andalusian scholar most noted for his commentaries on the works of Aristotle

Ibn Tufayl (too-FAYL), around 1100–85 • Author of a book called *Alive, Son of Awake*, considered one of the best works of literature of Andalusian Spain

Khadija (hah-DEE-jah), around 555–620 • A wealthy widow, she was Muhammad's first wife and his first convert to Islam

Al-Ma'mun (al-mah-MOON), 786–833 • An especially well-educated caliph who supported the philosophical religious scholars known as the Mutazilites

Mansa (MAHN-suh) **Musa** (MOO-suh), died 1337 • Mali's emperor from about 1312 to 1337; known for his 1324–25 pilgrimage in which he distributed gold as gifts all along the route to Mecca

Mansa (MAHN-suh) **Sulayman** (soo-lay-MAHN), died 1360 • King of Mali from 1337 to 1360, who supported Islamic teaching at Timbuktu

Al-Mansur (al-man-SUHR), 712–75 • Abbasid caliph from 754 to 775, who supported Persian literature at his court and founded Baghdad

Mehmed II (MEH-meht), 1432–81 • Ottoman sultan from 1444 to 1446, and again from 1451 to 1481; brought Byzantine Empire to an end in 1453 when he conquered Constantinople

Muawiyah (moo-AH-wee-yah), around 601–80 • Fifth caliph and founder of the Umayyad dynasty

Muhammad (moo-HAH-mud) **ibn Abdallah** (ub-duh-LAH) **al-Hashimi** (al-hah-SHEE-mee), around 570–632 • Founder of the Islamic religion, considered God's last and greatest prophet by his followers; united many Arab tribes and converted them to worshipping one God

Mutope (moo-TOW-pay), 15th century • King of Mwenemutapa around 1450–80; under his rule, Mwenemutapa grew to be the most powerful state on the Shona plateau

Mutota (moo-TOW-tah), 15th century • Last-known king of Great Zimbabwe, who conquered the northern Shona people and established the Kingdom of Mwenemutapa

Oduduwa (oh-DOO-doo-wah) • First man, according to the beliefs of the Yoruba people of West Africa

Olorun (oh-low-ROON) • Sky god to the Yoruba people of West Africa

Omar (OH-mahr) **Khayyám** (kai-YAHM), 1048?–31 • Persian poet best known for his collection of quatrains *The Rubaiyat*

Osman (os-MAHN), around 1259–1326 • Founder of the Ottoman Empire

Roxelana (rok-sih-LAH-nah), died 1558 • Wife of Suleyman the Magnificent

Rumi (ROO-me), **Jalal** (juh-LAHL) **ad-Din** (ud-DEEN) **ar**, 1207–73 • Persian poet

Sinan (see-NAHN), 1489–1588 • Chief architect under four Ottoman sultans

Sonni (SUH-nee) **Ali** (AH-lee), died 1492 • First king of Songhay Empire, ruling from about 1468 to 1492

Suleyman (soo-lay-MAHN) **the Magnificent**, 1494–1566 • Ottoman sultan from 1520 to 1566; he added many conquests to the empire, supported strict religious practices, defended Islam against heresy, and supported the arts

Sundiata (suhn-dee-AH-tah), 13th century • Fabled founder of the Kingdom of Mali, around 1235–50

Tariq (TAR-ehk), died 720 • Muslim general

Tunka (TUNG-ka) **Manin** (MA-nin), 11th century • King of Ghana, ruled around 1054–68

Umar (oo-MAHR), around 581–644 • Second caliph, from about 634

Uthman (OOTH-mahn), around 574–656 • Third caliph, from 644

SOME PRONUNCIATIONS

Al-Andalus (al-AHN-duh-LOOS)

Awdaghost (AW-duh-gost)

Axum (AHKS-oom)

Baghdad (BAG-dad)

Bambuk (bam-BOOK)

Benin (beh-NEEN)

Bitu (BEE-too)

Buré (boo-RAY)

Gao (GOW)

Ghana (GAH-nuh)

Great Zimbabwe (zim-BOB-way)

Hijaz (hee-JAHZ)

Ifé (EE-fay)

Jenne (jeh-NAY)

Kilwa (KIL-way)

Kumbi Saleh (KOOM-bee sah-LEH)

Maghrib (mah-GREEB)

Mapungubwe (MAH-pehng-GOO-bway)

Mecca (MEH-ka)

Medina (meh-DEE-nuh)

Pate (PAH-tay)

Sofala (soh-FAH-luh)

Yemen (YEH-mun)

enna

Balkan Constantinople
Peninsula (Istanbul)
Greece
Bursa• ANATOLIA
(TURKEY)
Black Sea
Caspian
Sea
Aral
Sea

ASIA

Indus River

Rhodes Cyprus Syria
Mediterranean Sea

•Aleppo
•Baghdad
Mesopotamia •Karbala
(Iraq) •Kufa
Palestine •Basra

Tigris River
Euphrates

PERSIA
(IRAN)

Sind

Damascus
Jerusalem•

Cairo•

ibya
Egypt

wila

sert

Nile River

Persian Gulf

Oman

Gujarat

SOUTH
ASIA

Arabian Sea

Sri Lanka

•Uhud
Badr•
•Medina
Hijaz
•Mecca

Red Sea

Arabian
Peninsula

ARABIA

AXUM
•Axum

AFRICA

YEMEN
•Aden

Congo River

•Mogadishu

Indian Ocean

Pate•
Lamu
•Malindi
•Mombasa
Zanzibar

•Mafia
•Kilwa

Zambezi River

MWENEMUTAPA

SHONALAND

Great
Zimbabwe•
Toutswe•
•Mapungubwe

•Sofala

Limpopo River

Madagascar

ahari

esert

0   400 mi
0   600 km

THE AFRICAN AND MIDDLE EASTERN

WORLD, 600—1500

INTRODUCTION
THE LAY OF THE LANDS

When they think of Africa, many people imagine a specific landscape. Maybe you picture a jungle dense with vines and darkened by heavy leaves. Or a vast grassland savannah where lions roam. Or miles and miles of desert where nobody lives and nothing grows. Africa is an enormous continent, so it has room for all of these environments, and more.

The Earth wears the Equator around its middle like a belt. Most continents fall either above or below this belt, but it runs right across the middle of Africa. The Equator is the hottest place on Earth, and it accounts in part for Africa's extreme landscapes, from dense rain forest to dry desert. Across the western equatorial center of the continent, the land is very hot and humid and it rains often, giving rise to dense forests. Hollywood movies often represent Africa as having jungles, but there are no jungles, just forests. As the forest spreads out from the Equator, both north and south, it gives way to grassland savannahs, which cover most of the continent. Most Africans live in the rain forests and on the savannahs.

Just north of the northern savannahs is a region called the Sahel, where it rains a little—just enough for some short grasses to grow. Across the Sahel, the landscape gradually changes from grassland into the Sahara, the world's largest desert. The desert, of course, gets no rain at all, but some things do manage to live there by getting water from the ground. On top of the Sahara, one of Africa's surprisingly few mountain ranges, the Atlas Mountains, divides the dry desert from the waters of the Mediterranean Sea.

Unlike what you see on the nature shows on television, Africa is not just rain forest and desert and grassland. It has thousands of miles of coastline, with the Atlantic Ocean in the west, the Indian Ocean in the east, and the Red Sea in the northeast. For centuries the coastline has connected Africans with people around the world. Port cities bustle with people from many places, who have gathered to trade not only goods and raw materials but also ideas, beliefs, and cultures. Across the Red Sea lies Africa's largest nearby neighbor, the Arabian Peninsula. Life on the peninsula is mostly like life in the Sahara Desert: hot, dusty, and dry. The Arabian Peninsula is in the middle of a region called the Middle East, which includes Egypt to the west and the lands of southwestern Asia (formerly known as Persia) to the east.

In the centuries after 600, the Middle East made a big impact on many Africans' religious beliefs, as a new faith called Islam spread westward from the Arabian peninsula. Islam took root fairly quickly among North Africans, especially in the port cities and lands that bordered the

The coast of East Africa is surpassingly beautiful, stretching from the southern part of modern Somalia to northern Mozambique. For more than 2,000 miles, there are sun-splashed white-sand beaches, coral-craggy river inlets, and gorgeous coral formations reaching offshore up to several miles.

Mediterranean and Red Seas. But it took longer to become a way of life in West Africa, where farmers' religious beliefs were tied firmly to their need for gods to protect their crops. And Muslims never traveled deep enough into southern Africa to spread their religion to that end of the continent at all.

At first glance, the lay of the land might not seem to matter much. The Arabian desert seems to be just a dramatic setting for stories about princes and flying carpets, genies and magic lamps. The African savannah seems nothing more than a backdrop for the fight between two wild animals onscreen that keeps you on the edge of your seat. But terrain has everything to do with how people live. For one thing, in medieval times deserts, seas, forests, and rivers helped to speed up or slow down the spread of trade, technology, ideas, and religious beliefs. For another, different natural features have given unique histories to different parts of the African and Middle Eastern worlds, affecting everything from what people ate, to how they got along, to the stories they told themselves to keep from being afraid of things they didn't understand. Only some of these histories have room to unfold in the pages that follow, but that's part of the fun of history—the more you explore it, the more you find to explore.

CHAPTER 1

CAMELS, CARAVANS, AND THE KA'BA

THE ARABIAN PENINSULA AROUND 600

It is near the end of the 6th century, and you are a young caravan guide who lives in the trading town of Mecca, in a hilly part of west-central Arabia called the Hijaz. Mecca is small, so small that you are one of only a few thousand people who live here. Like everyone else's, your house is made of brick and stone, with a flat top to deflect the rays of the hot Arabian sun. To keep cool you usually wear a long cotton gown. It fits loosely, so your sweat doesn't get too sticky, and it's white to reflect the sunlight away from your body. Your family draws its water, which is precious in this dry climate, from a well in the public square at the center of town.

Together with other members of a tribe called Quraysh, your family also goes to the square to worship at the Ka'ba, a sacred stone building that's just taller than your father. Nearly 350 idols—sacred statues and colored stones—are housed inside the Ka'ba. Later, the 9th-century Iraqi historian Hisham ibn Muhammad al-Kalbi will have this to say about you and your people: "The Arabs were passionately fond of worshipping idols. Some of them took unto themselves a temple around which they centered their worship, while others adopted an idol to which they offered their adoration." Even the courtyard that surrounds the Ka'ba is sacred and scattered with idols.

In the 6th and 7th centuries, buildings at Mecca and Yathrib probably resembled these flat-roofed structures built from stone and mud plaster. At that time, Arabia had no real cities and even fewer towns.

Byzantine merchants used bronze weights, such as these inlaid with silver, to provide a standard of weight for their transactions. In the 7th century, Byzantium was the most powerful state and its capital, Constantinople, the biggest commercial center in the Mediterranean world.

For hundreds of years, your region has been a bustling transit area between the Byzantine (Roman) and Sassanid (Persian) empires in the west and India and China in the east, wealthy lands that supply the westerners with luxury goods, such as spices, perfumes, and exotic silk and cotton textiles. The key to this trade is southwestern Arabia, in an area called Yemen. Unlike the rest of the peninsula, Yemen enjoys a regular rainfall. It has plenty of mountain streams, which have been dammed to supply water to grow grains such as wheat, as well as trees whose sap is used to make frankincense and myrrh, key ingredients in expensive incense and perfumes.

As a caravan guide, you go to Yemen's ports to meet traders who sail the Indian Ocean carrying luxury goods from East and South Asia to Mesopotamia, Palestine, Syria,

Arabia is a peninsula, surrounded on three sides by seas, in the southwest part of Asia. Temperatures are extremely hot, sometimes reaching 130 degrees Fahrenheit. Arabia gets almost no rain, so it is mostly waterless deserts and dry, treeless flatland, called steppes. Since people couldn't farm much, most of them relied on trade to make their living.

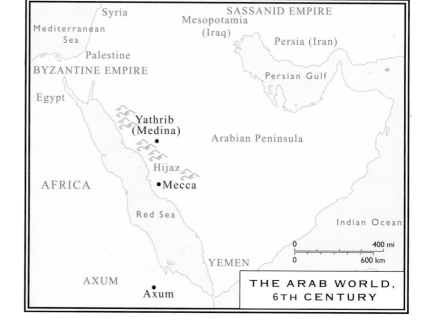

THE ARAB WORLD, 6TH CENTURY

and other lands that border the Mediterranean Sea. A Greek sailor of the 1st century wrote that Yemen's ports "teem . . . with Arabs—shipowners or charterers and sailors—and [they are] astir with commercial activity. For they share in the trade across the [Red Sea]." This is still the case in your times. Ships putting into these busy seaports from Africa and eastern lands empty cargoes of ivory, animal hides, rhinoceros horn, gold, incense, pungent spices, rich perfumes, and textiles dyed in brilliant hues.

Afterward, some of your fellow caravan guides transport these goods by camel along a route that runs northeastward to Persia. Meanwhile, you embark on a northerly route that goes to Egypt and Syria, where you will pass the merchandise to other traders, who will carry it onward to North Africa, Italy, and Byzantium.

The northern route, which passes through the Hijaz and your hometown of Mecca, is extremely dangerous. For one thing, the lands in the north of the Arabian Peninsula are better watered than most, so there's a lot of competition for them. This region has been at the heart of a long fight between the great Byzantine and Sassanid empires. Their continual wars have sapped the strength of these mighty realms until now they are both at the point of exhaustion. Because the pastureland is good in the north of Arabia, Arabian desert nomads have also moved into this hotly contested region. Nobody is ever completely in power, so bandits and robbers are free to run rampant. Some desert nomads, called Bedouin, who live in the neighborhood of Mecca attack and rob caravans as part of their livelihood.

These groves are in the interior, extending over a great tract of land, and there absolutely nothing else grows except palm trees. The Emperor Justinian had received these palm groves as a present from Abochorabus, the ruler of the Saracens there. . . . Formally, therefore, the emperor holds the Palm Groves, but for him really to possess himself of any of the country there is utterly impossible. For a land completely destitute of human habitation and extremely dry lies between, extending to the distance of a ten days' journey. . . . So much then for the Palm Groves.

—Procopius of Caesarea, *History of the Wars,* around 550

ON THE ROAD AGAIN——AND AGAIN

In their desert home, the Bedouin rarely get more than 10 inches of rain a year, and even that is undependable. So they must live as nomads, roaming from place to place, pitching their tents wherever there is water, and jealously guarding their wells from other tribes. Since they can't farm, the

continued on page 20

Meanwhile, in Africa

COSMAS INDICOPLEUSTES, THE CHRISTIAN TOPOGRAPHY OF COSMAS, AN EGYPTIAN MONK, 548

While different people struggled for power on the Arabian Peninsula in the 6th century, its African neighbor across the Red Sea, the Christian kingdom of Axum, enjoyed a position as a powerful state between the rival Roman Byzantine and Persian Sassanid empires. Axum had developed a thriving trade with merchants from Egypt, Greece, Rome, India, and Persia through their port of Adulis. An Egyptian Christian named Cosmas Indicopleustes visited the kingdom and wrote a book about it in 548. Here is what he had to say about Axum's trade with communities on the Red Sea coast and Yemen and of its unique way of trading for gold.

The region which produces frankincense is situated at the projecting parts of Ethiopia, and lies inland, but is washed by the ocean [the Red Sea] on the other side. Hence the inhabitants of Barbaria [the Red Sea coast], being near at hand, go up into the interior and, engaging in traffic with the natives, bring back from them many kinds of spices, frankincense, [cinnamon], [pen reeds], and many articles of merchandise, which they afterwards send by sea to Adulis, to the country of [Yemen], to Further India, and to Persia. . . .

The country known as Sasu [a province of the Axumite king-dom] is itself near the [Red Sea], just as the [Red Sea] is near the frankincense country, in which there are many gold mines. The King of the Axum-ites according[ly], every other year . . . sends thither special agents to bargain for the gold,

A southern Arabian farmer drives a team of two oxen. Unlike much of the Arabian Peninsula, Axum's trading partner Yemen in southern Arabia had good conditions for farming.

and these are accompanied by many other traders—upwards, say, of five hundred—bound on the same errand as themselves. They take along with them to the mining district oxen, lumps of salt, and iron, and when they reach its neighborhood they make a halt at a certain spot and form an encampment.... Within this they live, and having slaughtered the oxen, cut them in pieces, and lay the pieces on top of the thorns, along with the lumps of salt and iron. Then come the natives bringing gold in nuggets like peas, called *tancharas*, and lay one or two or more of these upon what pleases them—and then they retire to some distance off. Then the owner of the meat approaches, and if he is satisfied, he takes the gold away, and upon seeing this its owner comes and takes the flesh or the salt or the iron.

If, however, he is not satisfied, he leaves the gold, when the native seeing that he has not taken it, comes and either puts down more gold, or takes up

The first Axumites were the children of marriages between local Africans and Arab immigrants. By about the 1st century, the Axumites had developed their own styles of stoneworking, with elaborate windowlike carving. This tall, thin monument, more than 78 feet high and carved from solid rock, dwarfs the visitors in the lower right corner of the picture.

what he had laid down and goes away. Such is the mode in which business is transacted with the people of that country, because their language is different and interpreters are hardly to be found.

continued from page 17

Bedouin breed camels and goats. They're continually on the move to find new pastureland for their herds.

Bedouin love their camels the same way that later American cowboys love their horses. Camels are exceptionally strong—a camel can carry a great burden up to 100 miles and go for eight days without water. They are essential for long-distance transportation across the desert. They also supply milk that is made into camel cheese. When the Bedouin want meat, they slaughter a goat. They also breed horses, which are prized for their swiftness in battles.

The Bedouin occasionally trade their milk, cheese, meat, and skins with people who live in settled areas in exchange for crops and manufactured goods such as weapons, cloth, and saddles. They also supplement their living by raiding settled farmers, fellow nomadic tribes, and caravan traders like you.

These people of the desert celebrate strength, courage, and fighting skill. After battle, one 6th-century poet exclaims,

Hudhayl [the enemy tribe] is burned! I burned them!
I, fearless!

A peasant milks a goat in this mosaic from a Byzantine palace floor. Goat milk, as well as meat, was a crucial part of people's diets in the Middle Eastern world.

"Then I said, 'Drive him on! Let his reins go loose, while you

    turn to me.

Think not of the camel and our weight on him. Let us be happy.'"

      —Poem of Imru-Ul-Quais, from the wall of the Ka'ba,

      sometime before 622

I wearied when they were weary—
Whose spear drank a deep first draught, and liked it,
And drank again, deep of unfriendly blood.

Feuding and the need for revenge fan repeated skir-mishes. Few Bedouin can read or write, so they share stories or make up poetry about heroic deeds performed in their small, never-ending wars.

Proud of their personal honor and independence, the Bedouin are fiercely democratic. They dread letting any one person gather too much power. Their tribal elders (all men) usually meet to make important decisions, especially about military matters. Women are allowed to participate, but very rarely, usually when decisions involve marriage or child care. Every elder gets to speak his mind, and usually the opinions of the most eloquent men carry the most weight.

With so much warfare, however, strong leadership is critical to the welfare, even the survival, of the clans and tribes. Every tribe has a *shaykh,* meaning "elder," the leader whose opinions matter most in the tribal councils. He often makes crucial decisions for the tribe, though other tribal elders can reject them. His authority is based on the respect people feel toward him. Usually he is someone who comes from a clan that is noted for its leadership. The elders choose the *shaykh.* They always select a brave and strong warrior who knows how to lead others in battle.

The *shaykh* has to be a good diplomat, because he's responsible for negotiating agreements with other tribes. He

With the reins in his left hand, an Arab from the early part of the first millennium guides his camel. Camels were central to the nomadic Bedouin life, both for travel and as beasts of burden.

must also settle disputes among the tribal elders. He is generally someone who is wealthy by Bedouin standards, meaning he owns many camels and horses. He is known for sharing his food and livestock, particularly with fellow clanspeople whenever feasts are held. Since Bedouin men can have as many wives as they can afford, usually the *shaykh* has the most wives and children in the tribe.

GODS ON THE GO: WORSHIPPING IDOLS

Like most people of the time, Arabs believe there are many gods. The beliefs of the Bedouin tribes are what people today call polytheistic, that is, they associate gods, goddesses, or spirits with the things they find in nature, such as trees, rocks, streams, and springs. They worship idols and, like other tribes, have their own gods, goddesses, and objects they consider to be holy. According to al-Kalbi,

> Whenever a traveler stopped at a place or station [in order to rest or spend the night], he would select for himself four stones, pick out the finest among them and adopt it as his god, and use the remaining three as supports for his cooking-pot. On his departure he would leave them behind, and would do the same on his other stops.

Because the Bedouin are nomads, they don't have any permanent shrines. But there are a few places such as Mecca, with its Ka'ba, that do. According to al-Kalbi,

The person who was unable to build himself a temple or adopt an idol erected a stone in front of the Sacred House or in front of any other temple which he might prefer, and then [walked around] it in the same manner in which he would [walk around] the Sacred House. . . . The Arabs [had the habit of offering] sacrifices before all these idols . . . and stones. Nevertheless they were aware of the excellence and superiority of the [Ka'ba], to which they went on pilgrimage and visitation.

Religious Arabs tried to visit the Ka'ba at least once in their lifetimes.

Using their control of the Ka'ba as leverage, Mecca's Quraysh tribe convinced the Bedouin to allow safe passage to all caravans into and out of the city for one month of the year. This holy month when people would be guaranteed safe entry into Mecca to deposit their sacred idols and worship at the sacred shrine of the Ka'ba is called Ramadan. It is why there are so many idols around and inside the shrine. Each one belongs to a different tribe. With a break in the fighting at least once a year, people feel encouraged to trade in Mecca.

Although the Ka'ba is important to most, the people who live on the Arabian Peninsula don't share a common religion. Like other tribes, the Quraysh believe there are many gods, but they also accept that there is a chief God, whom they call Allah. Some tribes also worship goddesses, and some say these goddesses are the "daughters of Allah." Christians and Jews, who believe in only one God, have settled on the Arabian Peninsula too. To the south of Mecca, some Christians have established a monastery, a place where monks live and pray. Some Arab tribes have converted to Judaism. Some tribes at Yathrib, a community about 200 miles north of Mecca, are Jewish. Between local Bedouin bandits, Christians, Jews, and other tribes quarreling among themselves, and foreign Byzantines and Sassanids fighting wars, your life as a caravan guide on the peninsula is pretty chaotic. If only a single strong leader would emerge, maybe you and the other guides could finally trade in peace.

Wearing an elaborate crown of horns, a Sassanid king was immortalized in bronze sculpture sometime in the 5th or the 6th century. His family ruled Persia between 224 and 651, in a succession of 27 kings.

CHAPTER 2

THE MESSENGER OF ALLAH
MUHAMMAD AND THE BEGINNING OF ISLAM

Across the Red Sea from Yemen, in the mountains of the Horn of Africa, thrived a powerful Christian kingdom called Axum. Around 500, a king of Yemen had converted to Judaism and persecuted the Christians there, forcing many of them to leave their homes. The Axumites took revenge on the Yemeni king for tormenting their fellow Christians by seizing caravan trade routes and invading Yemen in 525. Around 570, the African troops tried to push farther into the Arabian Peninsula by attacking Mecca. They advanced riding on the backs of formidable elephants. According to Muslim tradition, a flock of birds defended Mecca by dropping stones on the Axumite army. Because the Axumites came on elephants, the Meccans call that year

This Turkish mosaic dates from the same century that the Axumite Ethiopians are said to have attacked Mecca on the backs of fearsome elephants.

the Year of the Elephant. That was the year Muhammad, the Prophet of Islam, was born.

Muhammad's father died shortly before the birth of his son. When he was five or six years old, his mother died too, leaving poor Muhammad an orphan. Luckily, his uncle Abu Talib took the little boy in and raised him.

Abu Talib was a merchant, and he taught his nephew the basics of trading. Muhammad worked as a caravan guide for a wealthy widow named Khadija. She was "intelligent and noble . . . the most distinguished of the women," according to the 9th-century historian of Islam, al-Tabari, and several men had proposed marriage to her. But, according to Muslim tradition, she herself proposed to Muhammad. According to al-Tabari, Muhammad had "deep black and large" eyes "and long eyelashes . . . his cheeks were smooth, and his beard was thick and long as if his neck were a silver pitcher." He is said to have been kind, especially toward women and children. When he was 25, Muhammad married Khadija.

Muhammad was very devoted to her and took no other wives while she remained alive, even though it was customary at the time for men to have several wives. Together the couple had eight children.

WANTED: PROPHET AND PREACHER

Muhammad had been born to a poor family, but he now became a prosperous trader. The obvious differences between

"And among His Signs is this, that He created for you mates from among yourselves, that you may dwell in tranquility with them, and He has put love and mercy between your [hearts]: verily in that are Signs for those who reflect."

—The Quran

A coastal region of western Saudi Arabia, the mountainous Hijaz extends along the Red Sea. According to his biographer Muhammad ibn Ishaq, the prophet Muhammad went to the mountains to meditate

rich and poor that he saw daily among the merchants troubled him. He developed the habit of leaving Mecca to climb into the low mountains outside the city to spend hours by himself in meditation and prayer. About the time he was 40 years old, while meditating in a cave near Mecca, he had a startling experience. Muhammad ibn Ishaq, his earliest biographer, records it like this (by "apostle of God," he means Muhammad):

[Muhammad] set forth to [Mount] Hira as was his [habit], and his family with him. When it was the night on which God honored him with his mission . . . Gabriel brought him the command of God. "He came to me," said the apostle of God, "while I was asleep, with a coverlet of brocade whereon was some writing, and said 'Recite!'"

Thus began the career of Muhammad as a prophet. By the time he died 22 years later, Muhammad had many more moments of inspiration during which Muslims believe he received messages from God. God's messages to Muhammad dealt with many topics, but they always repeated certain themes that Muhammad was told to preach to the Arabs. First, God told him there was only one God and that people were to cease worshipping other gods and idols. Second, Muhammad was warned of a Day of Judgment that would come when God would judge all people according to their obedience to God. The Quran (the written record of what God said to Muhammad) says that when Judgment comes, for all those who believe in God and do good works, "God has prepared a great reward and they have nothing to fear. They shall be served with silver dishes, and . . . cups brim-full with ginger-flavored water" and rewarded "with robes of silk and the delights of Paradise. Reclining there upon soft couches, they shall feel

Divine Message Received

**MUHAMMAD IBN ISHAQ, BIOGRAPHY OF
THE MESSENGER OF GOD, 8TH CENTURY**

*The earliest biographer of Muhammad, a man named Muhammad ibn Ishaq,
wrote the* Biography of the Messenger of God *in the 700s, and in it he
recorded how the Prophet received his first revelation. Muslims believe this is
when the Angel Gabriel visited him for the first time.*

[Muhammad] set forth to [Mount] Hira as was his [habit], and his
family with him. When it was the night on which God honored him
with his mission . . . Gabriel brought him the command of God. "He
came to me," said the apostle of God, "while I was asleep, with a coverlet of brocade whereon was some writing, and said 'Recite!' I said,
'What shall I Recite?' He pressed me with it so tightly that I thought
it was death; then he let me go and said to me again, 'Recite!' I said,
'What shall I Recite?' He pressed me with it again so that I thought
it was death: then he let me go and said, 'Recite!' I said, 'What shall
I Recite?' He pressed me with it the third time so that I
thought it was death and said 'Recite!' I said, 'What
then shall I Recite?'—and this I said only to deliver
myself from him, lest he should do the same to me
again. He said:

'Recite! in the name of thy Lord who created,
Who created man of blood [clotted].
Recite! Thy Lord is the most beneficent,
Who taught [people with] the pen,
Taught that which [they] knew not . . .
So I read it, and he departed from me.

*When Muhammad began preaching in the early 7th century,
some of his followers wrote down what he said on dried
bones. Wood and paper were scarce.*

It is not a matter of piety that you turn your faces to the East or West [in prayer]. Righteous is the one who believes in God and the last day, the angels and Scripture and the prophets; gives wealth, however cherished, to relatives and orphans, the needy and travelers and beggars, and for freeing slaves; and prays and gives zakat (donations or alms). And [the righteous] fulfill promises when they make them, and are patient in misfortune, hardship and trouble. These are the ones who are proven truthful and are pious.

—The Quran

there neither the scorching heat nor the biting cold. Trees will spread their shade around them, and fruits will hang in clusters over them."

As nice as all this sounded, at first Muhammad was badly frightened by the mysterious moments of revelation. When the angel told him to preach, he started in the circle of his family and friends. The faithful Khadija supported him and was his first convert. His best friend, Abu Bakr, and his cousin Ali converted too. Eventually, Muhammad was encouraged to begin telling his fellow Meccans of God's messages. Most of them did not believe Muhammad when he told them there was only one God, because this contradicted their ancient religion, which taught that there were many gods. But what really worried them was the threat that Muhammad's teachings and denunciation of their tribal idols posed for their religious shrine, the Ka'ba. Meccans also feared for the lucrative trade arrangements with neighboring tribes, who regularly visited this shrine and the idols it housed.

Muhammad did manage to convert a few of the rich Meccans. However, most of his converts were Mecca's poor people or slaves, whose welfare Muhammad taught was of utmost importance to God:

Known as Venus to the ancient Romans, Al-Uzza was the patron goddess of Mecca before the Meccans became monotheists, believers in a single god. Unfortunately for archaeologists, most pre-Islamic idols were destroyed.

Did he [God] not find you an orphan and give you shelter? Did he not find you lost on your way and guide you? Did he not find you destitute and enrich you? So then, do no wrong to the orphan, [nor] the supplicant do not turn away and make the grace of your Lord your constant theme.

Muhammad's followers came to be called Muslims, which means people who "submit to God." Angered by Muhammad's insistent preaching about one "Lord" and the just behavior God commanded, the majority of Meccans rejected the Muslims, ridiculing them and even beating and killing them, although Muhammad himself remained protected by his uncle Abu Talib and his family.

In 619, circumstances suddenly grew worse for Muhammad. His beloved wife, Khadija, died. Muhammad once said, "Every woman who dies, and her husband is pleased with her, shall enter into paradise." Then his uncle Abu Talib died. The loss of their love, support, and protection was hard for Muhammad.

THE MOVE TO MEDINA

Even while many Meccans had rejected his teaching, Muhammad had settled many disputes at Mecca. Yathrib, a

"When God sent his Prophet, who came preaching the Unity of God and calling for His worship alone without any associate, [the Arabs] said, 'Maketh he the god to be but one god? A strange thing forsooth is this.' They had in mind the idols [they had previously worshipped]."

—Iraqi historian Hisham ibn Muhammad al-Kalbi, *The Book of Idols,* 9th century town about 200 miles north of Mecca, had a number of tribes, three of them Jewish and the others polytheistic, that is, believing in the traditional tribal gods. For many years these tribes had been quarreling among themselves. So, because Muhammad had gained a reputation for fairness in settling disputes, the people of Yathrib invited him and his followers to settle there. According to Muslim tradition, once Muhammad understood that God had willed the move, they made the journey. This move, in 622, was known as the *hijra*, Arabic for "emigration." To Muhammad and his followers, the hijra represented their flight from the false religious beliefs of Mecca and its tribes to "true" religious beliefs in Yathrib, now called Medina, under Muhammad's direction. The *hijra* marks the beginning of the Islamic calendar.

In Mecca and Medina, as throughout Arabia, people lived by tribal rules. In Medina, however, Muhammad established an entirely new kind of society for Arabia, one based not on clan and tribe but on shared religious values. They formed a community (*Umma* in Arabic) based on a

The veiled women in this 17th-century fresco are following one interpretation of a verse in the Quran that reads, "If you ask [Muhammad's wives] for something, then ask them from behind a hijab [veil or curtain]." Muslims who believe that women should veil themselves base their view on this verse, considering the prophet's wives (he married several after his first wife, Khadija, died) to be role models for pious women.

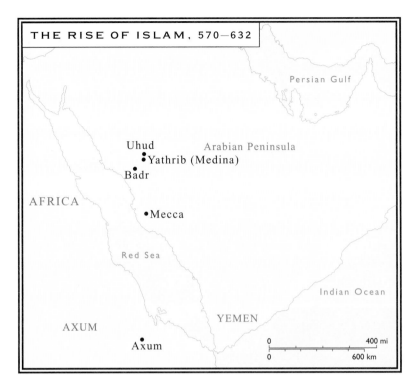

THE RISE OF ISLAM, 570—632

Persian Gulf

Arabian Peninsula

Uhud
Yathrib (Medina)
Badr

AFRICA

Mecca

Red Sea

Indian Ocean

YEMEN

AXUM

Axum

0   400 mi
0   600 km

belief they all shared that there is just one true God and that this God requires that they obey him in everything. The Quran states, "Those who have embraced the faith and fled from [Mecca], and fought for the cause of Allah with their wealth and their persons, and those [people of Medina] that sheltered them and helped them, shall be friends to each other." The community included Muslims and Jews. Both groups shared the belief that there is only one God. The Quran refers to the Hebrew Torah as the Word of God, and Muslims believed in the patriarchs and prophets of the Hebrew Bible. The Quran's story of the creation is the same one told in the Book of Genesis.

According to the constitution of Medina, dictated by Muhammad, each tribe was allowed to keep its tribal customs and religion, but all would cooperate in matters of defense, and disputes among them would be referred to Muhammad for arbitration.

The Muslims were joined together by their faith that God was speaking to them and telling them how to live

In 680, the Muslims erected the Dome of the Rock mosque in Jerusalem. The site is important to both Muslims and Jews. According to Muslim tradition, God removed Muhammad in his sleep to this spot, from which he flew into heaven. According to Jewish tradition, it is the place where God prevented Abraham from sacrificing his son Isaac.

through Muhammad. In Medina, away from clans and tribal rules, Muhammad was forced to take on new responsibilities. The heavenly messages continued right up to Muhammad's death, many of them directing the day-to-day lives of his growing community of believers, the Muslims. Muhammad's authority came from God, not the tribal elders. He used it to make treaties on behalf of the Muslims with other tribes and settle disputes among the Muslims, as well as between Muslims and members of other groups. He made military decisions and led his followers in war. The Quraysh tribe of Mecca continued to attack the Muslims. God ordered Muhammad and the Muslims to fight and subdue those who refused to live peacefully with them.

In a battle at the wells of Badr, in 624, Muhammad ordered his followers to ambush a caravan carrying goods the Meccans had taken from the homes of Muhammad's followers who had moved to Medina with him. The Muslims, though outnumbered, released a hail of arrows on the Meccans in the blinding desert sun. Having surprised and frightened the Meccans by the boldness of their charge, the Muslims routed their enemies. The victory lifted the spirits of the Muslims and strengthened their confidence in God and Muhammad.

The defeat at Badr angered the Meccans and made them resolve to wipe out Muhammad and his allies. The following year they sent an army of about 3,000 north to do just that, and a battle took place at a place called Uhud. This time the Meccans won a narrow victory. Rather than following up their victory by pursuing and finishing off the Muslims, however, the Meccans withdrew. The Quraysh and their Bedouin allies organized an even bigger force in 627 to try again to finish off the Muslims and their allies at Medina. Muhammad, who had received information that the Meccans were coming, ordered the Muslims to dig a ditch around the part of Medina where he expected the Meccans to attack in order to keep them from crossing into the city. For this reason, historians have called this event the Battle of the Ditch. The Meccan assault failed. The loss completely exhausted the Meccans. They just could not beat Muhammad.

They eventually worked out a truce, and in 630 Muhammad and the Muslims were allowed to go to Mecca and pray at the Ka'ba. Muhammad entered the Ka'ba and smashed all the images and idols it contained. The only piece that he allowed to remain was the Black Stone. Muhammad and his followers believed that this stone had been given to Abraham, the great patriarch of Jews, Christians, and Muslims, to build a shrine to God. From then on, the Quran required each Muslim to make the pilgrimage to the sanctuary in Mecca at least once in a lifetime.

By any measure, the final five years of Muhammad's life were highly successful. His defeat of the Meccans brought many converts to Islam, including most of the Quraysh tribe and their allies. Tribal leaders all over Arabia accepted God and paid allegiance to Muhammad as his messenger and the leader of the Muslims. Muslims believe that, in these final years, God and Muhammad laid out the Five Pillars of Islam. These are the basic duties that every Muslim must practice:

1. Give witness that "There is no other god but God, and Muhammad is the Messenger of God."
2. Pray five times a day—before dawn, midday, midafternoon, evening, and nighttime—in the direction of Mecca and the Ka'ba.
3. Give donations or alms to the needy.
4. Fast during the daylight hours of Ramadan, the 9th of the 12 months in the Muslim lunar calendar—no eating or drinking while the sun shines.

Today the Ka'ba stands nearly five stories tall at the center of a mosque in Mecca. But a 9th-century Muslim historian named al-Tabari tells us that before the 7th century "it consisted of loose stones rising to somewhere above a man's height, and they [the Meccans] wished to make it higher and roof it over."

5. Go to Mecca at least once in a lifetime to perform the rituals of pilgrimage, the most important of which is to pray at the Ka'ba.

Besides these Five Pillars, Muslims also had to follow rules about eating, such as avoiding pork or alcohol, since they believed that God forbade them. Gambling was also forbidden.

In 632, shortly after he had returned to Medina from his final pilgrimage, Muhammad suddenly became ill. After a very short illness, at the age of 62, he died. Muhammad's sudden, unexpected death, however, was not an end but a beginning—the beginning of the spread of the Islamic religion and civilization around the world.

CHAPTER 3

THE SWORD OF ALLAH
THE ISLAMIC EXPANSION

When Muhammad died suddenly in 632, the little Muslim community in Medina was in great distress. Its members urgently needed a new leader to keep them together. Muhammad had been God's final prophet—there was no way that mere people could replace a man chosen by God. They would need a different kind of leadership from now on. In some ways, Muhammad's leadership had been like that of a tribal *shaykh*—he made treaties with other tribes, settled disputes between fellow Muslims, made military decisions, and led his followers in war. A *shaykh* was generally chosen from among the members of just one family. Some Muslims believed that Muhammad had designated his son-in-law and cousin Ali as his rightful heir. However, most Medinans thought the new leader should be an elder who was close to Muhammad, someone with whom Muhammad had often shared his thoughts. These people wanted Muhammad's best friend, Abu Bakr, to lead them, and they won.

Abu Bakr was a plain, humble man and a faithful Muslim. In fact, he had been Muhammad's first male convert to Islam. According to Muhammad's 9th-century biographer, Abu Muhammad 'Abd al-Malik Ibn Hisham, who wrote down what he knew based on oral tradition about his accepting the position of leader, Abu Bakr respectfully declared, "O people, I have been appointed to rule over you, though I am not the best among you. If I do well, help me, and if I do ill, correct me." Abu Bakr knew he was no prophet, so he was content to be addressed simply as "leader of the believers." Later on, other successors called themselves deputy, or *caliph* in Arabic.

Abu Bakr lived for only two years after his friend Muhammad died. But, during those years, he accomplished a great deal. With Muhammad's death, some tribes that had

A 16th-century Egyptian artist painted a diagram of the sacred city of Medina on this tile. The mosque that Muhammad and his followers built dominates the top part. Muhammad's burial site is at the bottom. Middle Easterners call the date palm tree (lower right) the "Tree of Life." It is a holy symbol to Muslims.

converted to Islam thought that their political alliance with Medina was over. But Abu Bakr would have none of that. According to Ibn Hisham, he asserted that "If any people hold back from fighting the holy war for God, God strikes them with degradation. If weakness spreads among a people, God brings disaster upon all of them." Under his leadership, the Muslims forced the quitters back into the Islamic fold. They also convinced most of the tribes of Arabia to join them and conquered the rest. It helped that the tribes were divided. They didn't stand a chance in the face of Muslims united by religious zeal and the sheer determination of Abu Bakr. It also helped that the Muslim community was prospering. Many tribes wanted to share in the wealth.

Muslims believed that, through Muhammad, God had told them it was their duty to extend Islamic rule. They were convinced that only Islam promised to protect human dignity and allow people to live up to their potential. So they called on communities that weren't Muslim to either accept Islam or make a treaty promising to protect the rights of Muslims and live peacefully with them. If non-believers refused to accept these offers, then Muslims considered them a threat to Islam. In these cases, the Muslims believed that war was justified. "Going to war is prescribed for you," reads the Quran, "though it is for you a hateful thing. Yet it may well be that something you hate is nevertheless good for you, just as it can happen that you set your heart on what is bad for you. Knowledge in these things is God's, not yours." The Muslims also believed that if you died fighting in a jihad, that is, a holy war fought in the name of God, you were guaranteed a place in heaven on the

Day of Judgment. The Quran told them so: "[Muhammad] and the believers with him took up the jihad with their property and their persons. Theirs are the good things: they are the ones who attain success. God has made ready for them gardens with flowing streams in which they forever abide in the great triumph of bliss."

UMAR RULES

To continue spreading Islam after Abu Bakr died, the Muslim leaders at Medina chose another close companion of Muhammad, Umar, as the next caliph. Abu Bakr had brought all of Arabia under Muslim rule. Umar's mission was to expand Islamic rule beyond the peninsula's borders. These expeditions posed tough challenges. The mighty Byzantine and Sassanid empires controlled the territories to the north and northeast of Arabia. For the first time, Muslim raiders came up against trained professional soldiers.

Nevertheless, with shouts of "God is great!" they struck out of the desert wastes like lightning on their swift little steeds, with their curved, razor-sharp swords flashing doom. The Byzantines and Sassanids had been fighting each other for nearly a century, and by 634, their troops were exhausted. It didn't hurt that these empires had also taxed their subjects heavily and persecuted Jews and non-orthodox Christians, who were delighted to be free of their Byzantine or Sassanid rulers.

A Sassanid king grabs the wrist of the Roman emperor, who raises his sword as they do battle on horseback. The Sassanids and Byzantines wore each other out with their constant warfare.

Umar made some calculations and divided the Muslims into two armies. One pressed north into Byzantine territory. The other he sent northeast into lands held by the Sassanids, who weren't paying much attention. Umar's advances caught the imperial powers completely off guard. With surprising speed and ease, the Muslims took victory after victory, often with the help of former Roman or Persian subjects. Between 634 and 651, they swept over all their enemies, finally defeating the Byzantine army in 643 and the last Sassanid king in 651. The Muslims now controlled a stretch of territory that reached nearly 3,000 miles from Libya and Egypt in the west to almost the borders of India in the east.

The Muslims had not entirely defeated the Byzantines, however. There were pockets of resisters, and the Muslims had to keep up the pressure on them. With swarms of captured and hastily built ships, the Muslims harassed Byzantine fortifications on the Mediterranean islands of Cyprus, Rhodes, and Sicily. The Arab tribesmen had had no experience with naval warfare, but they were quick learners. Constantinople, the capital of the Byzantine Empire, was the grand prize. Twice in the 7th century, major naval expeditions besieged the city. But Constantinople's exceptionally high walls locked the Muslims out. The Byzantines kept the Muslim fleets at bay with something

Victory at Yarmuk

**AHMAD IBN-JABIR AL-BALADHURI,
THE ORIGINS OF THE ISLAMIC STATE, 9TH CENTURY**

*The Battle of the Yarmuk between the Muslims and the Byzantines was central
to the expansion of the Islamic state in the century after Muhammad died.
The subjects of the Byzantine emperor were of many faiths, and the Christian
Byzantines often discriminated against them. So their anger toward the
Byzantines played a role in the Muslim victory. Ahmad ibn-Jabir al-Baladhuri
was a historian who lived in the 9th century, several hundred years after
the battle. He spent most of his life in Baghdad studying and enjoyed great
influence at the court of the Abbasid caliphs. Here is his account of the
Muslim victory at Yarmuk.*

When Heraclius massed his troops against the Muslims and the
Muslims heard that they were coming to meet them at al-Yarmuk,
the Muslims refunded to the inhabitants of Hims the *kharaj* [tribute]
they had taken from them saying, "We are too busy to support and
protect you. Take care of yourselves." But the people of Hims replied,
"We like your rule and justice far better than the state of oppression
and tyranny in which we were. The army of Heraclius we shall
indeed, with your 'amil's' help, repulse from the city." The Jews rose
and said, "We swear by the Torah, no governor of Heraclius shall
enter the city of Hims unless we are first vanquished and exhausted!"
Saying this, they closed the gates of the city and guarded them.

The inhabitants of the other cities—Christian and Jew—that had
capitulated to the Muslims, did the same, saying, "If Heraclius and his
followers win over the Muslims we would return to our previous condition, otherwise we shall retain our present state so long as numbers
are with the Muslims." When by Allah's help the "unbelievers" were
defeated and the Muslims won, they opened the gates of their cities,
went out with the singers and music players who began to play, and
paid the *kharaj*.

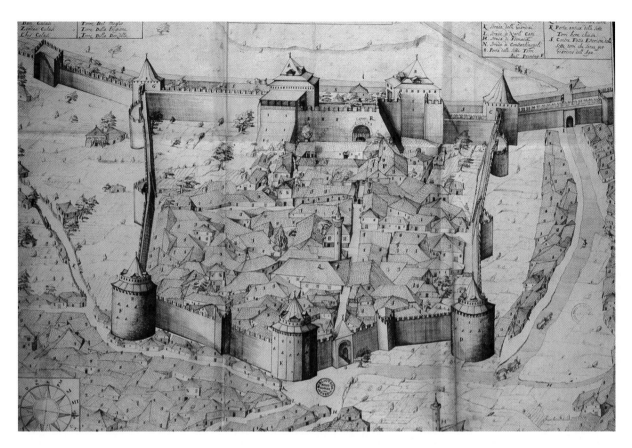

Tall, thick walls connected Constantinople's seven heavily fortified towers. For centuries after the rise of Islam, the Byzantine city's barricades defended eastern Europe against Islamic expansion.

called "Greek fire," a mystery weapon that has puzzled historians for a long time. It seems to have been an oily substance that the Byzantine Greeks ignited and hurled onto Muslim ships.

THE SMELL OF WATER

As the Muslim navy kept pressing against the Byzantines in the north, Muslim armies were marching westward across North Africa to the shores of the Atlantic Ocean. There, they encountered North African Berbers, tribal nomads as fierce in combat as they were. Traveling with their flocks, taking whatever they could from the land, North Africa's Berber tribes were masters of the Sahara Desert. An old African saying goes that a Berber guide could smell water from miles away and tell exactly where he was just by tasting the sand. Whether this story was true or not, the Berbers had remarkable survival skills. They had to—the air in the Sahara was (and still is) dry, dusty, and hot, not good for farming and settling down. The 1st-century BCE Roman geographer Strabo had written that the Berbers "wander from place to place with their flocks. . . . Their flocks and herds are small in size, whether sheep, goats, or oxen; the dogs also, though fierce and quarrelsome, are small."

The Arabs called the Berber homeland the Maghrib, or "the West," since it lay west of the Arabian Peninsula. Muslim armies conquered what would become Tunisia in 665, and Algeria and Morocco in 680, but frequent Berber revolts drove the Arabs right back out. Conquest was easy, but holding on to those conquests proved very hard with a people who prized their independence. The Berbers refused to be ruled by foreigners. They considered themselves to be not much different from their Muslim conquerors.

And in many ways, they weren't different. Large Berber tribes, such as the Sanhaja and the Tuareg, led nomadic lives very much like the Bedouin of Arabia. They too depended on their camels to trek across the vast desert sands. Like the Bedouin, the Berbers lived off the livestock that traveled with them from place to place. According to Strabo's *Geography*, "They have no oil, but use butter and fat instead. . . . They live also upon the flesh and blood of animals, milk, and cheese." But unlike the Bedouin, who

"*[The Berbers] belong to a powerful, formidable, brave and numerous people; a true people like so many others the world has seen—like the Arabs, the Persians, the Greeks and the Romans.*"

—Tunisian historian Ibn Khaldun, *Muqaddimah*, 1377

wore long gowns to protect themselves from the harsh sun, the Berbers had a different dress code for dealing with the heat. Strabo wrote that they "are for the most part naked."

The Sahara was not all Berbers roaming through the rock and sand and heat, however. There were also oases, places with natural springs and deep wells that invited people to settle around them. Little islands of green basking in the desert sun, oases were where farmers lived. Although the people of the oases were like other Berber peoples—speaking Berber languages and having the same olive skin and straight hair—they were not nomadic. They didn't live in tents, but in houses made from stone. Usually they were friendly with the desert nomads, but at other times, when the desert people's food supplies ran low, they raided the oases for food, water, livestock, and sometimes even women and children whom the nomads forced to live as slaves. Strabo reported that the Berbers "live on millet and barley, from which also a drink is prepared. . . . There are no fruits, except the produce of trees in the royal gardens." The variety of fruit may not have been great, but the one that the Berbers grew most was a prized delicacy: dates.

Although the Berbers rejected Arab rule, they generally accepted Islam. The simplicity of the Islamic religion appealed to them. From North Africa, they helped to spread the Muslim conquest to the north and west, into Chris-

A Berber woman in a desert oasis miraculously makes a date palm yield fruit just by touching it. Middle Eastern traders introduced the date palm, one of their region's oldest tree crops, dating back to more than 5,000 years, to northeast Africa and the eastern Mediterranean.

tian Spain, which the Arabs called al-Andalus. In 711, a general named Tariq and his Berber band crossed the Mediterranean Sea from Morocco to Spain, claiming a hill (*jabal* in Arabic) that still bears his name: the Rock of Gibraltar (the "tar" is from *Tariq*). As they prepared to meet the Spaniards, Tariq rallied his men:

> Oh my warriors. . . . Behind you is the sea, before you, the enemy. You have left now only the hope of your courage and your constancy. . . . Remember that if you suffer a few moments in patience, you will afterward enjoy supreme delight. Do not imagine that your fate can be separated from mine, and rest assured that if you fall, I shall perish with you, or avenge you.

He went on to tell his warriors,

> The Commander of True Believers . . . has chosen you for this attack from among all his Arab warriors.

Berber villagers used plentiful local stone to construct the walls of this village, perched on the hilly, rocky slopes of Tunisia's Atlas Mountains. Like the village dwellers of Arabia, the Berber tribes of North Africa lived in small villages where they cultivated wheat and raised livestock such as camels, sheep, and goats.

Spectators in Tunisia (on the North African coast) enjoy watching a chariot race, a favorite Roman pastime. Before Islam and the Arabic language came to Africa's Mediterranean seaboard, people there spoke Latin, the language of the ruling Roman Empire.

. . . The one fruit which he desires to obtain from your bravery is that the word of God shall be exalted in this country, and that the true religion shall be established here. The spoils will belong to yourselves.

Within a few years, Tariq and his men had taken much of the Spanish peninsula. Arabs followed them, and soon both Berbers and Arabs ruled Spain. By 716, all of Spain was in Muslim hands. Pushing ever northwards, they set their sights on France. Muslim armies drove farther and farther north until, in a decisive battle fought near Tours, France, in 732, the Frankish general Charles Martel commanded an army that defeated the Muslims and finally stopped their advance into Europe.

CHAPTER 4

MANAGING THE EMPIRE
ISLAM GROWS INTO AN EMPIRE OF FAITH

The explosive growth of Islamic rule from a tiny community in Medina to an empire posed enormous administrative challenges for the caliphs and the Muslims. For one thing, Muslim conquerors were not allowed to confiscate property. But they had to settle somewhere. The caliph Umar's solution was to restrict the Muslims to living in military camps. Soon, many of these camps developed into full-blown cities. Another challenge was taxation. The caliph set up a central treasury at Medina to take care of these funds. According to the third pillar of Islam, Muslims were required to pay a charitable tax called *zakat*, which went toward supporting the community. But there was no system in place for taxing people of other faiths. So the treasury collected a special tax, called the *jizya*, from non-Muslim populations of the conquered lands.

The military camps that Umar set up to keep Muslims separate from the local populations grew into full-blown cities. Among these were Basra in Iraq, Cairo in Egypt, and, in this 17th-century view, Damascus in Syria.

For a while, everything worked smoothly. However, strains soon began to divide the Muslims. Some Muslims rejected the use of their taxes in Medina rather than where they lived, and some non-Muslims thought their taxes were too high. The 9th-century historian al-Tabari wrote,

> Umar . . . went out one day to stroll in the market-place, and he met . . . a slave . . . and he was a Christian. [The slave] said, "O Commander of the Faithful, help me against . . . a great tax . . . imposed upon me." "How much is your tax?" asked Umar. "Two dirhams every day," he replied. . . . "I do not consider your tax great," said Umar.

Three days later, according to al-Tabari, the angry Christian slave stabbed Umar to death.

Leaders in Medina had elected the first two caliphs, Abu Bakr and Umar, without incident, but the choice of the third caliph, Uthman, was more controversial. People who chose him liked that he was a member of the Umayyad clan, whose men were known for being expert managers. The Muslims needed an excellent administrator to oversee their growing empire. Others Muslims, however, resented Uthman because the Umayyads had been some of Muhammad's bitterest opponents at Mecca. But Uthman himself actually had been one of the few members of his clan to convert before Muhammad left Mecca for Medina. Still another faction continued to support Ali, Muhammad's cousin, sticking to the position that one of Muhammad's close relatives should lead the Muslims.

FAMILY FAVORITES AND BITTER FACTIONS

With an empire that had grown very large, Uthman needed skillful administrators whom he knew he could trust. The natural choices to fill the highest positions were his highly capable Umayyad relatives. Uthman made his cousin Muawiyah the governor of Syria. This favoritism for family members infuriated Uthman's opponents. In 656, a faction of troops from Egypt cornered Uthman in his house at

Because Islamic law forbids the artistic portrayal of human beings, ornate writing of passages from the Quran was the main form of artistic expression among Muslims for many centuries. Passages from the Quran could even be made to resemble birds and animals. This one is in the form of a hoepoe bird.

Medina. A party of hotheads among them forced their way into his house, and when his wife tried to stop them, they severely wounded her. Coming upon the old caliph while he was reading his Quran, they stabbed him to death. For the first time a caliph had been murdered at the hands of other Muslims.

Despite such hatred from some factions, Uthman left Muslims a very important gift. Some of Muhammad's original followers had written some of the messages he received from God on pieces of dried bone or parchment. People also remembered the sacred words by committing them to memory and reciting them. But different dialects led to different readings, so Uthman had all the verses collected and written down, and he ordered any inaccurate words to be destroyed. He published the complete collection in 653, three years before he died, and Muslims have followed this official version of the Quran ever since.

After the murder of Uthman, Ali was selected as caliph at last. He was chosen for his wisdom and piety, although

A highly devout Muslim, Uthman holds a Quran and prayer beads in this 18th-century Muslim painting. Although his father opposed Muhammad, the third caliph, Uthman, was an early convert to Islam.

some people thought it was his relationship with Muhammad that qualified him. Those people, who came to be called the *shi'ah* ("faction" in Arabic) of Ali, or sometimes simply as Shiites, considered him to be Muhammad's first legitimate successor. They used the term "imam," which means leader, rather than "caliph," to describe Ali.

Uthman's cousin Muawiyah, the Syrian governor, accused Ali of failing to punish Uthman's assassins. Muawiyah, moreover, thought that it was his turn to be caliph. The armies of the two men met in a battle in 656 at a place in Iraq called Siffin. Although Ali's troops were vastly outnumbered, the battle was close. Muawiyah's troops asked for a ceasefire so that the two sides could talk out their differences. Ali agreed.

For Ali, things took a turn for the worse when some of his supporters refused to stand by him. They believed that

"*Our belief concerning the Alawiya [descendants of Ali] is that they are the descendants of the Messenger of God and devotion to them is required.*"

—Creed of the Shiite theologian Muhammad ibn Ali ibn Babawayh (Sheik al-Saduq), 10th century

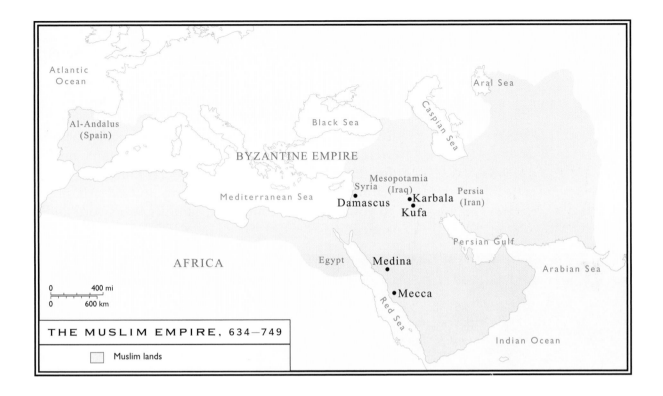

Atlantic Ocean

Al-Andalus (Spain)

Aral Sea

Black Sea

Caspian Sea

BYZANTINE EMPIRE

Mediterranean Sea

Syria
Damascus

Mesopotamia (Iraq)
•Karbala
Kufa

Persia (Iran)

Persian Gulf

AFRICA

Egypt

Medina

Arabian Sea

Mecca

Red Sea

Indian Ocean

| 0 | 400 mi |
| 0 | 600 km |

THE MUSLIM EMPIRE, 634–749

Muslim lands

Ali had offended God by negotiating rather than letting God decide the winner through battle. According to al-Tabari,

> [Some of the men] met together and . . . then said, "By God it is not fitting that a people . . . should prefer this world to the commanding of good . . . and the proclaiming of truth. . . . So let us go out, brethren of ours, from this settlement [Ali's camp] whose people are wicked to one of the districts of the mountains or to one of the towns rejecting these innovations that lead [us] astray."

These troops abandoned Ali's camp and, from the Arabic word *kharaj*, which means "to exit," became known as the Kharijites. They went on a rampage through southern Iraq, killing innocent people and seizing their possessions. Ali was forced to kill most of them to stop their pillaging. Some of the rest escaped.

ALI'S END

Five years later, one of them took his revenge on Ali. According to an eyewitness account,

> By God I was performing the prayer ritual in the great mosque on that night when Ali was stabbed. I was among a large number of men of [Kufa] who were praying near the door . . . when Ali came out for the morning prayer . . . I noticed something glitter and I heard, "Authority belongs to God, Ali, not to you or your accomplices," and I saw a sword and a second.

Ali's assassination would mark the death of the last elected caliph.

Ali's rival Muawiyah succeeded him in 661, and from that time until 750, all the caliphs came from his family, the Umayyads. Throughout the Umayyads' rule, the empire began to crack under the weight of old rivalries among the Arab tribes. Tribes in Syria supported Muawiyah and his successors, so Muawiyah moved the capital from Medina to Damascus. The assassination of Ali, rather than discouraging his supporters, the Shiites, had deepened their distrust and

The treasury of the Umayyad dynasty was housed in a building called the Bayt al-Mal, built in 715. Just beyond the treasury is one of the three towers that were Islam's first minarets, the towers from which muezzins, or callers, summoned the faithful to prayer.

Most Magnificent Mosque in the World

" **IBN BATTUTA, TRAVELS IN ASIA AND AFRICA, 14TH CENTURY**

Moroccan traveler Ibn Battuta was a 14th-century Muslim who traveled most of the known world at that time. His many years of wandering took him from Spain to China and from Constantinople to Kilwa, East Africa. In his trave-logue, he described the great mosque built by the Umayyad caliphs in Damascus, Syria.

[The Great Mosque in Damascus is] the most magnificent mosque in the world, the finest in construction and noblest in beauty, grace and perfection; it is matchless and unequalled. The person who undertook its construction was the Caliph Walid I [705–715]. He applied to the Roman Emperor at Constantinople, ordering him to send craftsmen to him, and the Emperor sent him twelve thousand of them. The site of the mosque was a church, and when the Muslims captured Damascus, one of their commanders entered from one side by the sword and reached as far as the middle of the church, while the other entered peaceably from the eastern side and reached the middle also.

So the Muslims made the half of the church which they had entered by force into a mosque and the half which they had entered by peaceful agreement remained as a church. When Walid decided to extend the mosque over the entire church he asked the Greeks to sell him their church for whatsoever equivalent they desired, but they refused, so he seized it. The Christians used to say that whoever destroyed the church would be stricken with madness and they told that to Walid. But he replied, "I shall be the first to be stricken by madness in the service of God," and seizing an axe, he set to work to knock it down with his own hands. The Muslims on seeing that followed his example, and God proved false the assertion of the Christians.

resentment toward the Syrians and Egyptians who supported the Umayyads. The Umayyad caliphs had to put down one rebellion after another in the eastern parts of the Islamic empire.

Muslims were also divided over how a caliph should be chosen. The Kharijite faction (one of whom had assassinated Ali) believed that the caliphs should be chosen for their righteousness. After all, the caliphs were "the deputies of God's Messenger." Kharijites were upset that Muawiyah and the succeeding caliphs were chosen because of their membership in the Umayyad clan rather than by election. From this time onwards, the majority of Muslims who followed the caliphs as their legitimate rulers, and who did not join the Kharijites and the Shiites in opposing them, came to be called the Sunnis.

Other Muslims, mostly pious believers, criticized the Umayyad caliphs for ruling too much by force. Muawiyah himself had restored peace to the Islamic empire through a combination of diplomacy and, when words failed, the use of raw military power. Too often, these pious Muslims pointed out that the Umayyads and the governors they appointed used harsh and uncalled-for methods against their opponents. Islam was supposed to bring peace and security to all, but oppression seemed to replace God's commands that people deal with each other justly and in obedience with His laws.

Shiite beliefs developed during the early decades of Umayyad rule. Many believed that before he died, Muhammad expressly had chosen Ali to succeed him as the rightful leader of his community but that his followers ignored his wishes and chose Abu Bakr (and later Umar and Uthman) instead. Following Ali's murder, many Shiites backed Ali's sons, Hasan and Husayn. In 680, while Husayn was on his way from Medina to Kufa, in Iraq, an army sent by the Umayyad caliph in Damascus ambushed and killed him near a village called Karbala. Al-Tabari reported: "All al-Husayn's followers were killed, among whom were more than ten young men from his family. An arrow came and struck his son while he had him in his lap." Husayn then

A man of the tribe of Madhhij killed [al-Husayn] and cut off his head. He took it to Ubaydallah [the governor of Iraq] and said:

Fill my saddlebag with silver and gold,
For I have killed the well-guarded king.
I have killed the man of noblest parents,
And when people trace descent his is the best.

[Ubaydallah] sent him to . . . Mu'awiyah [the Caliph] and with him he sent the head . . . [Mu'awiyah] began to poke the mouth with a cane . . .

[Someone] cried out to him, "Take your cane away. By God! How often have I seen the Apostle of God kiss that mouth!"

—al-Tabari, description of the killing of Muhammad's grandson al-Husayn, *The History of al-Tabari,* 9th century "took out his sword and fought until he was killed. A man of the tribe of Madhhij killed him and cut off his head. He took it to [the caliph's governor in Iraq]."

This event, more than any other, hardened Shiite feelings against the caliphs and the Muslim majority who supported them. Even today, Shiites consider Husayn to be a martyr and hold his tomb at Karbala, Iraq, to be sacred. On the anniversary of his death, they reenact his murder.

Another group the Umayyads had to contend with was non-Arab converts to Islam. Islam had become popular in some areas of the traditionally Christian Byzantine Empire. Byzantine emperors had forced their subjects to accept only one kind of Christianity—theirs. But Christians in Egypt, Syria, and North Africa often disagreed with the emperor's doctrines and were imprisoned and even tortured by Byzantine officials for their beliefs. When the Muslims

Jesus washes the feet of his disciple Peter in this 8th-century Italian mosaic. Muslims believed in Jesus as a prophet and in his disciples as helpers in doing God's work, which linked Islam with Christianity.

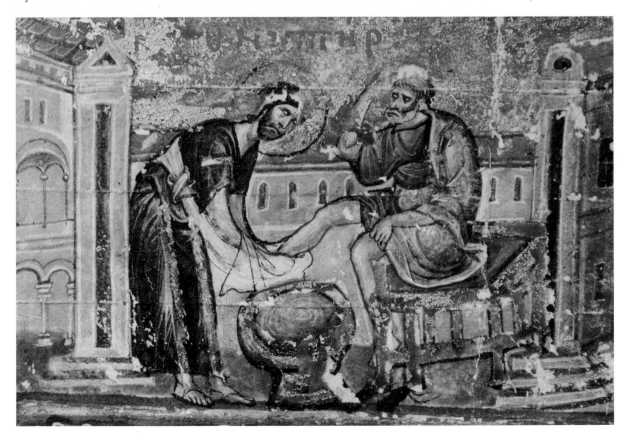

Two lions attack each other head-on on this ornate ivory perfume box from Spain. The ivory used to make this container probably came to Spain from the Umayyad caliph's Berber allies in Morocco, in northern Africa.

conquered these regions, Christians found Muslim rulers to be more tolerant than Byzantines. Islam was similar enough to their Christian beliefs to make conversion easy. Christians and Muslims both shared beliefs in only one God. They also believed in the Bible as sacred scripture, the patriarchs and prophets of the Old Testament, and a Final Day when God will judge each and every person, sending those who believe in Him and do good works to heaven and those who go against God's will to hell. Furthermore, Muslims revered Jesus as a prophet.

Unfortunately, however, the system Umar had created separated Arabs and Muslims and tended to favor them. Some Arab tribes simply accepted these converts as *mawalis* (Arabic for "dependents"), which legalized their status as Muslims but did not ensure equal treatment. Arab Muslims treated *mawalis* as second-class Muslims, because the caliph's officials continued to collect the *jizya* from them. Of course, this discrimination made the *mawalis* extremely angry with the Umayyad caliphs.

The *mawalis* got even with the Umayyads by throwing their support behind the Shiites in their opposition to the Umayyad caliphate. A Shiite rebellion that had begun in far eastern Iran swept westward, gathering *mawali* troops along the way. The revolution swept the Umayyads out of Damascus in 750 and established a new clan as caliphs. However, it did not quite finish off the Umayyads. Spain was their new destination, and there they set up a second caliphate.

CHAPTER 5

THE HOUSE OF ISLAM
THE FIRST WORLDWIDE CIVILIZATION

Most Muslims made their pilgrimage to Mecca, then turned around and went right back home. But not Ibn Battuta, who had made the 3,000-mile journey from his native Morocco. Besides all of the Middle East, he visited many out-of-the-way places, such as the African kingdom of Mali, the East African city of Kilwa, Delhi in India, the Maldive Islands in the Indian Ocean, Malacca in Malaysia, and even China, covering a grand total of about 75,000 miles. Most remarkable of all, everywhere Ibn Battuta went, fellow Muslims welcomed and entertained him. By the 1300s, you could travel from Spain to Southeast Asia and never leave the Dar al-Islam, or "House of Islam," as Muslims called Islamic lands.

THE ABBASID EMPIRE, 763

☐ Abbasid Empire at its largest extent

With the support of Persian *mawalis,* who were tired of being treated like second-class citizens by the Umayyads, a group called the Abbasids had ridden to victory against the Umayyad armies in 749–50 and declared themselves the new caliphs. When the Abbasids took over, they wanted to make Islam a way of life around the world, as well as a religion that respected every believer. They stopped collecting the unfair *jizya* (tax) on non-Arab Muslims. At the same time, the Abbasids cut off support payments to all Arab tribes except members of Muhammad's own clan and their descendants. Gradually, they replaced Arabs in privileged positions in the government and the army with Muslims from other cultures, especially Persians. Ability and religious piety came to matter more than race or cultural background under the new caliphs.

BUILDING BAGHDAD

The third Abbasid caliph, Abu Jafar al-Mansur, had felt that a new government needed a new capital. In 662, he decided that the best spot was in Iraq, on the banks of the Tigris River, because it was near the geographic center of the empire. The place was called Baghdad. Al-Mansur built a huge palace complex shaped like a wheel, with the caliph's mansion and personal mosque at its center. In his *History,* al-Tabari described al-Mansur's choice of the place for his new capital and the construction of the city:

> The city was built round so that, if the king settled in the middle of it, he was not nearer one place of it than another. He set up four gates on the model of military camps in war, and he built two walls, the inside wall being higher than the outside one. He built his palace in the middle of it and the congregational mosque next to . . . the palace.

The caliph may have had a great sense of architectural design, but apparently he was also a penny-pinching cheapskate. Al-Tabari further reported, "When al-Mansur had finished building his palace in the city, he entered it and

An Abbasid caliph built this mosque and spiral minaret, the tower from which Muslims are called to prayer, in the 9th century. The crier who called the faithful to prayer, called a muezzin, would climb the spiral staircase on the outside of the minaret. After making five rounds of the building, he would find himself in a circular room about 20 feet in diameter near the top.

toured it and approved of it and examined it and admired what he saw in it, except that he thought that he had spent too much money on it. . . . [He] demanded [from the builder] more than six thousand dirhams . . . , and he arrested him for it and [jailed] him, and he did not leave the palace until he had paid it [back] to him."

In the years after Baghdad was built, the city grew rapidly, radiating outward like the spokes of a wheel around the palace complex at its center. In their new city, great Abbasid caliphs developed a style of governing that proved to be even more colorful and domineering than that of the Umayyads. To match the majesty of their courts, they no longer were content with simple ways of being addressed by their subjects. The earliest caliphs such as Abu Bakr had been satisfied with "leader of the believers," but by the time of the Abbasids, caliphs preferred more lofty titles like "The Shadow of God on Earth."

The City of Palaces

YAQUT BIN ABDALLAH AL-HAMAWI, GEOGRAPHICAL DICTIONARY, 13TH CENTURY

This is an account of Baghdad written by Yaqut bin Abdallah al-Hamawi, a Greek by birth who was captured as a young man and taken to live in Baghdad as a slave. In 1199, he was freed, and between 1212 and 1224, he compiled his Geographical Dictionary. His account of Baghdad was based on 10th-century sources, so in reality it describes the city as it was in its glory days.

The city of Baghdad formed two vast semi-circles on the right and left banks of the Tigris, twelve miles in diameter. The numerous suburbs, covered with parks, gardens, villas and beautiful promenades, and plentifully supplied with rich bazaars, and finely built mosques and baths, stretched for a considerable distance on both sides of the river. In the days of its prosperity the population of Baghdad and its suburbs amounted to over two million! The palace of the Caliph stood in the midst of a vast park several hours in circumference which beside a menagerie and aviary comprised an enclosure for wild animals reserved for the chase. The palace grounds were laid out with gardens, and adorned with exquisite taste with plants, flowers, and trees, reservoirs and fountains, surrounded by sculptured figures. On this side of the river stood the palaces of the great nobles. Immense streets . . . traversed the city from one end to the other, dividing it into blocks or quarters, each under the control of an overseer or supervisor, who looked after the cleanliness, sanitation and the comfort of the inhabitants.

Baghdad was a veritable City of Palaces, not made of stucco and mortar, but of marble. The buildings were usually of several stories. . . .

Both sides of the river were for miles fronted by the palaces, kiosks, gardens and parks of the grandees and nobles, marble steps led down to the water's edge, and the scene on the river was animated by thousands of gondolas, decked with little flags, dancing like sunbeams on the water, and carrying the pleasure-seeking Baghdad citizens from one part of the city to the other. Along the wide-stretching quays lay whole fleets at anchor, sea and river craft of all kinds. . . .

These caliphs developed a system of government that reached from one end of their empire to the other. To make it work, they installed a royal post office and a spy network that reached throughout the empire. They employed translators so that leaders of the various lands they ruled could communicate with each other. And they surrounded themselves with legions of officials. They had divided the empire into many provinces and installed a governor at each province. At the head of this administration was the grand vizier, or chief adviser to the caliph at Baghdad.

Perhaps the largest category of officials was the hundreds of religious scholars whom the caliphs put on the state payrolls to see to it that their subjects were practicing the principles of the Sharia (Islamic law as established in the Quran) and the Sunna (Islamic customs based on Muhammad's divinely inspired actions). Among these men were scores of legal scholars, judges, prayer leaders, and market inspectors whose job was to enforce Islamic rules for honesty and the conduct of trade.

The market inspectors must have had a huge job, because trade was booming during the Abbasid caliphate. From the industrial centers of Baghdad and other major cities, trade routes linked the Islamic empire, reaching from Central Asia and even Scandinavia in the northeast, Morocco and Spain in the west, and African lands in the south, to Malaysia and even China in the east. Overland caravan routes reached from Aleppo and Damascus in Syria to China and from Cairo and the cities of North Africa to West Africa. Most shipping, however, was by sea. Muslims largely controlled the major Indian Ocean sea lanes from ports in East Africa, southern Arabia, western India, and Malaysia. Ibn Battuta described the port of Aden in southern Arabia in his *Travels in Asia and Africa*: "Its inhabitants are all either merchants, porters, or fishermen. Some of the merchants are immensely

The Abbasid caliphs minted their own coins, called dinars. This solid gold dinar *from the time of the third Abbasid caliph is more than 1,200 years old. The center reads, "Muhammad (is) the envoy of God," and the rim is inscribed with the words, "In the name of Allah."*

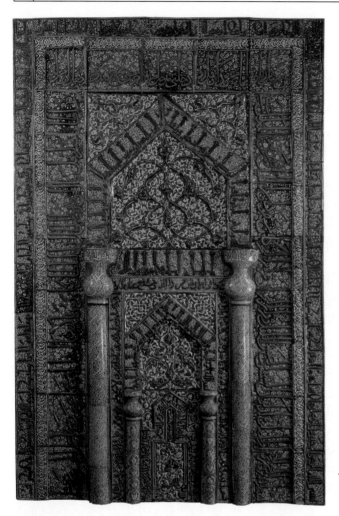

Most mosques have a mihrab, a prayer alcove built into the wall in the direction of Mecca, toward which Muslims pray. Thirteenth-century Persian ceramic makers made this mihrab by fitting glazed tiles into an elaborate pattern of calligraphy, flowers, and geometric shapes.

rich, so rich that sometimes a single merchant is sole owner of a large ship with all it contains, and this is a subject of ostentation and rivalry amongst them."

Alongside Islam, this far-flung trade network helped to hold the caliphs' empire together. Without doubt, the Abbasid caliphs oversaw the greatest empire in the world at that time, and it showed in the lavish way they lived. Their capital at Baghdad was the greatest consumer of goods in the entire empire. Caliphs lived in huge palaces decorated with ornate carvings in stone and wood; they hung the walls with carpets and textiles from both East Asia and the looms of their own craftsmen. They reclined on luxurious pillows and cushions covered in cloth made of gold and silver thread and adorned with precious stones. The caliphs, their families, and court officials dressed in cottons and silks woven with intricate inlays of precious metals and jewels. One Muslim scholar recorded that, at his death, the caliph Harun al-Rashid owned:

4,000 [robes] of variegated silk said . . . to have been woven with gold;
4,000 [robes] of . . . silk lined with the fur of the sable, the marten and other animals;
10,000 shirts and chemises;
10,000 qaftan;
2,000 trousers of different materials;
4,000 turbans;
1,000 wraps of different stuffs;
1,000 hooded robes;
5,000 handkerchiefs of different materials;
1,000 girdles, . . . described as studded with gold;

> 4,000 pairs of . . . boots, most of them lined with the fur
>   of the marten, sable, and other animals;
> 4,000 pairs of stockings.

Of course, he would have had plenty of servants to keep his room picked up.

To supply the demand for such luxury goods, industries sprang up all around the palaces of the caliphs and their representatives both in Baghdad and in the provincial capitals of the empire. In Baghdad and the cities of Persia, Ibn Battuta would have smelled the exquisite perfumes and walked on the gorgeous wool carpets they produced. Throughout Iraq and Persia, he would have seen craftsmen manufacturing pottery to rival the porcelains of China. In Egypt, he might have bought superior linen and wool textiles. In the cities of Syria, he probably drank from the most exquisite glassware and ate off the most delicate plates. And these were just a few of the industries that thrived in the Muslim empire.

Like Ibn Battuta, the craftspeople who made these wonderful things had a lot of freedom in their lives, especially in where they lived, traveled, and worked. People of the same profession lived in the same neighborhood, which was usually behind a wall. So if you wanted to buy a carpet, for example, you would walk through the gate into the neighborhood where the carpet makers worked at their looms. The largest cities had craft guilds, professional associations that regulated training programs for young potters, jewelers, cobblers, weavers, dyers, metalsmiths, carpenters, and stone masons.

The carpet maker's wife was expected to maintain her modesty around visitors and other strangers. She would certainly wear a veil in front of a stranger such as yourself. Her primary duties were to rear her children and look after her household (in some places, she might have been the owner of the home). As a side job, she might have

A luxurious wardrobe didn't spoil the 8th-century caliph Harun al-Rashid, beautifully attired in this 17th-century Indian miniature. An especially just ruler, he would disguise himself and go out at night, wandering the streets and bazaars of Baghdad to hear the talk and to ask people questions to see if they were being fairly treated.

"The eastern part has an abundance of bazaars, the largest of which is called the Tuesday bazaar. On this side there are no fruit trees, but all the fruit is brought from the western side, where there are orchards and gardens."

—Ibn Battuta, description of Baghdad, *Travels in Asia and Africa,* 14th century

Elaborately decorated with enamel paint, this Persian bowl features at its center a princess riding on an elephant. Simple Islamic pottery became much more refined as craftsmen responded to a wave of luxury goods that Arab and Persian merchants imported from China.

a craft that she could work on at home, such as weaving cloth. She sent her children to Quran school when they were around seven. They'd have three years to memorize the whole book. Afterwards, her son would begin a long training apprenticeship in his father's carpet shop. Her daughter would help her with household chores, learning how to run a home of her own one day.

The carpet maker's wife probably had a Slavic or African slave to help her with the household duties, and her husband may have had a slave-craftsman working in his shop. Some slaves were so prosperous they also had slaves. While visiting Damascus, Syria, Ibn Battuta was impressed to see how well Syrians treated their domestic slaves:

One day as I went along a lane in Damascus I saw a small slave who had dropped a Chinese porcelain dish, which was broken to bits. A number of people collected round him, and one of them said to him, "Gather up the pieces and take them to the custodian of the endowments for utensils." He did so, and the man went with him to the custodian, where the slave showed the broken pieces and received a sum sufficient to buy a similar dish. This is an excellent institution, for the master of the slave would undoubtedly have beaten him, or at least scolded him, for breaking the dish, and the slave would have been heartbroken and upset at the accident.

In some places, however, slaves, especially Africans, had to endure treatment as harsh as slaves have had to endure anywhere. During the 9th century, southern Iraqis forced East African slaves to drain malaria-infested swamps. The high death rates among them finally drove them to revolt.

REVOLTS AND REBELLIONS: KHARIJITES AND SHIITES

Abused slaves were not the only people to revolt. The Abbasids faced frequent rebellions by Kharijites and Shiites. The Kharijite movement attracted Muslims who opposed the hereditary control of the caliphate by just one family. Most of them were fanatics who believed that anybody, even a Muslim, who violated any of God's commandments automatically deserved to be killed as an unbeliever. Mainstream

This enormous Persian carpet, measuring 17 by 34 feet, is one of a pair that weavers worked in 10 colors of silk and wool. Each carpet has more than 25 million knots in it. It was made for a Persian king and used in a Muslim shrine.

Muslims rejected this position. Still, in the three centuries after the murder of the caliph Ali at the hands of a Kharijite, pockets of Kharijite resistance to authority continued in parts of southern Iraq, Oman (southeast Arabia), and northern Africa. Oman was especially stubborn in its opposition to the caliphs. In 751–52, the caliph Abu'l-Abbas sent a mighty force there to suppress a rebellion led by a tribal leader by the name of al-Julanda. The historian al-Tabari described the fighting that occurred:

> [T]hey fought a sharp engagement. . . . [The Abbasid general commanded] his followers to fix tow [a material like straw] on the end of their spears and soak this in naphtha [a flammable material] and set fire to it, and then go with these and set fire to the dwellings of al-Julanda's followers. . . . They did this and set fire to the houses. While the Kharijites were busy saving them and their children and families who were in them, [the Abbasids] pressed the attack and laid on their swords, meeting little resistance from them. Al-Julanda was one of those slain, and the number came to ten thousand.

The Abbasids were even tougher on the Shiites. Like Kharijism, Shiism appealed to people who were opposed to the ruling family. The Abbasids themselves had begun with

"There is a clue which [God] presents to you from your own relationships. Would you . . . regard the slaves in your hands as participants with you [in your religion], as if you and they were equals respecting it? Do you hold them in the same sort of respect that you have for one another?"

—The Quran

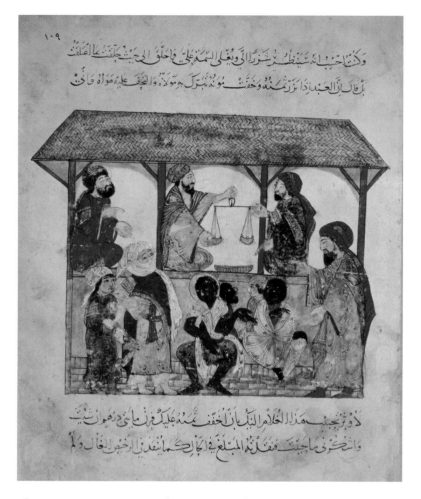

At a slave market, two Arab traders weigh out payment on a pair of scales while African slaves below wait to be sold. Islam did not forbid slavery, but the Quran encouraged Muslims to show kindness and, whenever possible, to convert their slaves and grant them their freedom.

Shiite support against the Umayyads. But once they were in power, the Abbasids wanted to lead all Muslims, not just the Shiite minority. They turned their backs on the party of Ali and crushed the Shiite leaders. Shiism then changed into a secret underground movement.

Not all Shiites shared exactly the same views, but they were all united in their firm belief that only the direct descendants of Muhammad's daughter Fatima and his son-in-law and cousin Ali had the knowledge to lead the Muslim community. Shiites believed that Muhammad had revealed a hidden meaning of the Quran to Ali and that Ali had handed down the secret knowledge only in their family. They called the rightful leaders imams. When the 11th descendant of Ali died in 874, Shiites believed he had left a son, Muhammad, who disappeared mysteriously from a cellar in Iraq. They believed this 12th imam then went into spiritual "hiding" and that someday he would return to create a perfect world. During the Abbasid period, most Shiites were not Arab but Persian.

By the late 9th century, Abbasid governors in Egypt, North Africa, Spain, and the farthest regions of Persia realized that they could rule without reporting to Baghdad. They declared their independence from the Abbasid capital and even established their own dynasties. Worse yet for the Abbasids, two rival families claiming to be the "true" caliphs surfaced during the 10th century. One of these was the Umayyad clan, some of whose members had escaped the massacre at Damascus when the Abbasids seized the Syrian city in 750 and had gone on to establish an independent caliphate in Spain. A Shiite dynasty called the Fatimids, after Fatima (Muhammad's daughter and Ali's wife), set up another rival caliphate in Egypt in 969.

To deal with these open acts of defiance, the caliphs were forced to rely more and more on Turkish slave armies. The Turks were superior soldiers and very skillful at fighting from horseback. The Abbasid caliphs' dependence on them made the caliphate even weaker, as the Turkish generals became more and more powerful in Baghdad. Finally, beginning in 1040, large numbers of a tribe of Turks, called the Seljuks, migrated from their homelands in Central Asia seeking new pasturelands. They captured Baghdad and in 1055 established the Seljuk sultanate (a region ruled by a sultan, a ruler without religious authority).

Luckily for the Abbasid Muslims, the Turks had converted to Islam and were not interested in destroying their empire. The caliphs got to keep their position as the religious leaders of the Muslims, while the Seljuk sultans took over political power. Muslims still honored the caliphs as their spiritual leaders,

Muslim artisans carved this delicate flask from rock crystal that was probably imported from a Swahili city in East Africa. Carving rock crystal was a specialty of craftsmen in Cairo.

but the caliphs barely enjoyed a morsel of political power.

Despite its weakened state, the Abbasid caliphate in Baghdad held on for another 250 years. The end finally came in the 13th century when the great Central Asian warriors called Mongols swept down from the north and destroyed the great cities of Persia. In an act of defiance, the last caliph refused to negotiate a peace settlement with the Mongol general, Hulegu, grandson of the great Mongol conqueror Genghis Khan. Refusal to negotiate infuriated the Mongol general. In 1258, his army overran Baghdad's defenses and the city was almost totally destroyed. Hulegu's army slaughtered hundreds of thousands of people and reportedly built a pyramid from the skulls of scholars and poets. Libraries and mosques, houses and palaces—all were burned. By the time Ibn Battuta arrived in Baghdad in the 14th century, he could report,

> The western part of Baghdad ... is now for the most part in ruins. In spite of that there remain in it still thirteen quarters, each like a city in itself and possessing two or three baths. The hospital is a vast ruined edifice, of which only vestiges remain.

In addition to Mesopotamia and Persia, the Seljuk empire included Syria. A Syrian potter made this Seljuk horse and rider in the 12th or 13th century, just before their empire fell to another tribe of expert horsemen, the Mongols.

CHAPTER 6

LIVING BY THE RULES
ULAMA AND PHILOSOPHERS

In the centuries before printing, scribes copied the Quran by hand and decorated the manuscripts with ornate designs. This 9th-century page uses an ancient form of Arabic writing, called Kufic script, which disappeared from use after the 10th century. Modern Arabic uses a much more fluid script.

After Muhammad's death, Muslims felt at a loss. Without his example of piety in everyday actions, they weren't quite sure how to express their faith in their daily lives. Even religious scholars disagreed about how they should act. Muslims considered Muhammad to have been the perfect Muslim, a man who was constantly inspired by God. Although they could never dream of matching his perfection—after all, God himself had inspired the things that Muhammad said and did—they could at least be good Muslims by trying to imitate his life. Muhammad had left them the Quran as a spiritual guide. But the Quran stresses moral principles and guidelines about piety and justice. It provides only a few detailed instructions about ordinary living.

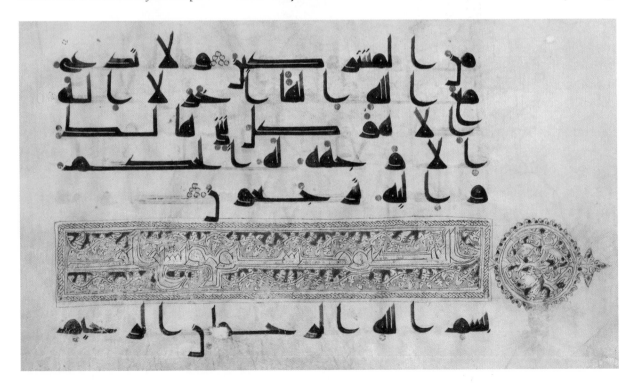

At first, it seemed that Muhammad's example of how to live had died with him. But Muhammad's companions helped their fellow believers to carry on by repeating hadiths, or accounts about things Muhammad had said or done. One hadith teaches Muslims how to greet each other in a proper Muslim manner: "You will not enter Paradise unless you are kind to each other, unless you warmly say salam [Peace] to each other whenever you meet." In another hadith, Muhammad instructs, "O Muslims, O fathers and mothers, O my followers, be kind and compassionate towards children, for someone who is not kind to children has no place among the Muslims." The hadiths form the basis of the Sunna, that is, the body of established Islamic customs and beliefs based on the living example provided by Muhammad. Taken together, Muhammad's example in the Sunna and God's divine word in the Quran teach Muslims how to live by their faith.

The great Abbasid caliphs encouraged discussion and debate of both the Quran and the hadiths, in order to give their Muslim subjects the spiritual guidance that they were seeking. They also employed experts on Islamic law to serve as judges in courts set up to enforce Islamic rules. These experts, called *ulama,* settled all sorts of issues, relying on collections of hadiths about Muhammad to resolve questions that the Quran did not address. In the courts, *ulama* discussed disputes over everyday affairs such as divorce, inheritance, trade, and property. They also made decisions concerning guilt or innocence, much as modern courts do, in more serious matters such as adultery, personal injury, theft, and murder. Only Muslims were allowed to testify against Muslims. Judges punished offenders with fines, imprisonment, beatings, and cutting off their hands, ears, or, in the most severe cases, heads.

RELIGION AND REASON

The religious scholars were not the only thinkers that the Abbasids encouraged. They also supported other scholars, such as translators and interpreters of ancient Greek texts.

"[A]ccording to the ancients, religion is an imitation of philosophy. Both . . . give an account of the ultimate end for the sake of which man is made. . . ."

—10th-century Muslim philosopher al-Farabi

Some of these scholars tried to make Islamic religious teachings fit the strict rules of logic, that is, the art of reasoning. They believed that because it would be unjust for God to want humans to sin and because God is just, God must give humans free will to choose or reject sinful behavior for themselves. These thinkers, called Mutazilites, refused to believe people didn't control their ultimate destiny.

This position was the opposite of that of other religious scholars who believed that because God is all-knowing, God knows beforehand if a person will sin. Some Muslims felt that the Mutazilites' attempt to make Islam follow the rules of logic violated their religion, and they were offended by some of the Mutazilites' conclusions, which they considered to be too radical. The most controversial of these was the Mutazilite notion that the Quran could not be eternal, as the *ulama* argued, because only God is eternal. This view angered many ordinary Muslims as well as the *ulama* because it seemed to diminish the Quran as the Word of God.

Nevertheless, the 9th-century caliph al-Ma'mun supported the Mutazilites. Al-Ma'mun himself was well read in philosophy and logic and sympathized with their views. What's more, he believed that as caliph he was wiser than ordinary Muslims and that it was his duty to decide what beliefs were acceptable. In a letter to his governors, al-Ma'mun claims,

> God has made incumbent upon the . . . caliphs of the Muslims that they should be zealous in establishing God's religion, which He has asked them to guard

faithfully; in the heritage of prophethood of which He has made them inheritors; in the tradition of knowledge which He has entrusted in their keeping.

In order to make the Mutazilite view the official Muslim position, al-Ma'mun forced many leading *ulama* to swear to the doctrine that the Quran was not eternal. But al-Ma'mun had one problem. The most highly respected religious scholar of the age, Ahmad ibn Hanbal, refused to take the oath. Al-Ma'mun couldn't just imprison or kill the great ibn Hanbal. The scholar's supporters would only rebel against the caliph. Without ibn Hanbal's support, there was nothing al-Ma'mun could do to firmly establish Mutazilite

Muslim scholars revered the ancient Greek philosopher Socrates, who is surrounded by his pupils in this 13th-century Turkish miniature. Greek philosophy had a strong influence on early Islamic theology and philosophy.

His Arrogance Knows No Bounds

" AL-TABARI, HISTORY OF AL-TABARI, 9TH CENTURY

In this letter, written to his governors, the caliph al-Ma'mun claims that he, as caliph, is responsible for ensuring correct beliefs among all Muslims. Most Muslims of his time probably would have agreed with him. However, his conceited tone is very apparent, and without a doubt, it contributed to his decision to impose an investigation in support of the Mutazilite philosophers against ulama *such as Ahmad ibn Hanbal. Throughout the letter he refers to himself as the "Commander of the Faithful."*

God has made incumbent upon the . . . caliphs of the Muslims that they should be zealous in establishing God's religion, which He has asked them to guard faithfully; in the heritage of prophethood of which He has made them inheritors; in the tradition of knowledge which He has entrusted in their keeping; in acting justly with the government of their subjects; and in being diligent in obeying God's will in their conduct towards those subjects.

The Commander of the Faithful has realized that the broad mass and the overwhelming concentration of the base elements of the ordinary people and the lower [levels] of the commonality are those who, in all the regions and far horizons of the world, have no far-sightedness, or vision, or faculty of reasoning by means of such evidential proofs as God approves along the right way which He provides. . . . [These persons are] a people sunk in ignorance and in blindness about God, plunged into error regarding the true nature of His religion and His unity and faith in Him . . . [they are] a people who fall short of being able to grasp the reality of God as He should be recognized . . . and to distinguish between Him and His creation . . . all this arises from the fact that they consider as perfectly equal God Himself and the Quran which He has revealed . . . and have asserted unequivocally as eternal and primordial, not created nor originated nor in any way by God.

views. In the end, his failure diminished both his religious authority and that of the Abbasid caliphs after him.

On the other hand, this dispute greatly strengthened the *ulama* as the true authorities on all matters concerning religion. But even the *ulama* found logic to be useful. In their quest to find hadiths to supplement the Quran, they used logic to test the truthfulness of the oral traditions they collected. They also rejected reports that couldn't be traced back to someone who knew Muhammad personally and then carefully recorded all the reports from trusted sources. By the 10th century, they had assembled thousands of hadith reports, checked their authenticity, and written them down.

Taken together, these reports became known as the Sunna, which Islamic legal scholars turned to for guidance if they couldn't find an answer in the Quran. If neither the Quran nor the Sunna provided a solution, the legal scholars could turn to the community for an agreement on a particular problem. If all else failed, experts in the Quran and Sunna rigorously examined them for similar situations that could be used as examples in the new case. This process kept Islamic law flexible enough to deal with changing circumstances, down to the present day.

SUFISM TAKES SHAPE

The Five Pillars and the Holy Law gave Islam its overall structure. But any religion based only on following rules, even God's rules, would not by itself be spiritually uplifting for everyone. Almost at the very beginning of Islam itself, some Quran reciters, called Sufis, had found chanting the poetic language of their holy book to be a good way of focusing on God. In addition to chanting, some Sufis tried to get closer to God by giving up all personal possessions, living as wandering beggars, and wearing only rough woolen (*suf*) garments. They believed that they might experience God by discarding all thoughts about earthly existence. Some Sufis spent much of their time alone, reading the Quran, chanting it out loud while swaying forwards and backwards. They took refuge in caves or in the homes of

With a thin white scarf draped across his shoulders, a Sufi worshipper sits on the ground hugging his knees, perhaps enjoying a quiet moment in the presence of his God.

*Come and be Love's
    [God's] willing slave,
for Love's slavery will save
    you.
Forsake the slavery of this
    world
and take up Love's sweet
    service.
The free, the world
    enslaves,
but to slaves Love grants
    freedom.
I crave release from this
    world
like a bird from its egg;
free me from this shell that
    clings.
As from the grave, grant
    me new life.
O Love, O quail in the free
    fields of spring,
Wildly sing songs of joy."*

—Jalal ad-Din al-Rumi,
    a 13th-century Sufi poet,
    using the language of love
    to express the bliss of
    being absorbed by God

anyone generous enough to give them shelter.

Many Sufis also found that by focusing on the idea of God while chanting and controlling their breath, they could achieve a state of spiritual ecstasy. In this state, they usually lost all awareness of themselves and believed they had become absorbed into God. While journeying through Iraq by caravan in the mid-1300s, the Moroccan traveler Ibn Battuta stopped at a town called Wasit, where he witnessed just such a Sufi spiritual exercise. He arrived at "an enormous monastery," where the Sufis began to dance "after the mid-afternoon prayer drums and kettledrums were beaten. . . . After this they prayed the sunset prayer and brought in the meal, consisting of rice-bread, fish, milk and dates. After the night prayer they began to recite their litany."

In Islam's early centuries, the *ulama* frowned on this unconventional practice. Some even hounded and harassed Sufis. This persecution finally stopped, though, in the 12th century when a highly respected scholar by the name of Abu Hamid Muhammad al-Ghazali convinced many *ulama* that Sufism did not violate God's laws. In fact, he pointed out, Sufi spiritual exercises inspired people's love of God. Such love only made them better Muslims. Al-Ghazali's success at convincing the *ulama* of Sufism's value led many Muslims to practice it. In the end, Sufis even helped to expand the Islamic world beyond Arabian and Persian borders into Africa and South and Southeast Asia. Many Africans and South Asians worshipped their gods and spirits through dance or music, playing instruments such as drums, tambourines, or xylophones. Since the Sufis accepted many of these practices, they made becoming a Muslim easier for people who performed them.

Sufis gradually organized themselves into associations, called *tariqas*. These associations usually admitted only men but were otherwise very permissive about the kinds of practices they allowed. Some *tariqas* engaged in extreme feats of physical endurance to demonstrate their spirituality. Using a combination of music, dancing, and rapid breathing, they'd work themselves into a trancelike state and sometimes perform incredible feats. Ibn Battuta describes one such scene in his travelogue: "A number of loads of wood had been brought in and kindled into a flame, and they went into the fire dancing; some of them rolled in it and others ate it in

By paving the way for music and dance in Islamic religious practice, Sufis helped to spread their faith to regions where music was important to native rituals. Indonesian youths dance to an orchestra of percussion and string instruments. Today, Indonesia is the largest Muslim country in the world.

their mouths until they had extinguished it entirely." He also wrote that some of them "even take large snakes and bite their heads with their teeth until they bite them clean through." But even though each of these Sufis expressed his spirituality in a different way from Ibn Battuta, they all shared the same faith through their commitment to the Five Pillars and Islamic laws and learning.

Sufis dance themselves into a state of spiritual ecstasy, as musicians play in the lower right of this painting. Such Sufi ceremonies were designed to put the participants into a trancelike state in which they might experience the nearness of God.

CHAPTER 7

HOUSES OF WISDOM
ISLAMIC ARTS AND SCIENCES

A hadith from Muhammad says, "The search for knowledge is a sacred duty imposed upon every Muslim." The Abbasid caliphs took this instruction as seriously as any of the Prophet's teachings. At that time, the most advanced medical, scientific, and mathematical knowledge came from the ancient Greeks, Indians, and Persians. Therefore, the caliph Abu Jafar al-Ma'mun, who reigned from 813 to 833, organized a research institute in Baghdad called the House of Wisdom, which was dedicated to the study of Greek, Indian, and Persian texts and their translation into Arabic. Soon, the best scholars of all backgrounds, Muslims and non-Muslims alike, from all over the Islamic world were participating in what became history's first center of advanced research.

Muslim scholars embarked on their own research as well, and until about the 10th century they continued to make great discoveries in philosophy, mathematics, medical studies, astronomy, chemistry, and physics. Abu Ali Hasan Ibn al-Haitham, who became known in the West as Alhazen, was a particularly outstanding Muslim physicist and math-

Scientists from around the Islamic world gather for a meeting in this illustration from a 15th-century manuscript. The Islamic world employed more scientists, produced more scientific texts, and supported scientific pursuits for a longer stretch of time than any other civilization before it.

ematician. He experimented with the way light separated into different colors when it passed through a prism. From such efforts, he speculated on the nature of light, and he applied his knowledge to studies of the eye. He was the first person to describe the parts of the eye and to provide a theory about how vision works.

MEASURING THE EARTH: ASTRONOMY, MEDICINE, AND THE SCIENCES

The Muslim physician Abu Bakr Muhammad ar-Razi studied and wrote about human anatomy and many diseases. A careful and observant doctor, ar-Razi may have been the first person to associate hay fever with pollen when he noted that people always seem to sneeze in the springtime, around "the time of the roses." By carefully monitoring patients with more serious ailments, he discovered that smallpox and measles were two different diseases. He focused more on providing treatment than developing theories, however. Ar-Razi tried new techniques to see what worked, but he fought against quacks, believing that doctors should be professionals. "Ignorant doctors are killers," he declared. When ar-Razi, always a practical man, became the director of a new Baghdad hospital, he reportedly determined where to build it by hanging meat around various parts of the city. A few days later, he inspected the meat and figured that wherever he found the least amount of decay would be the healthiest part of the city—and the best location

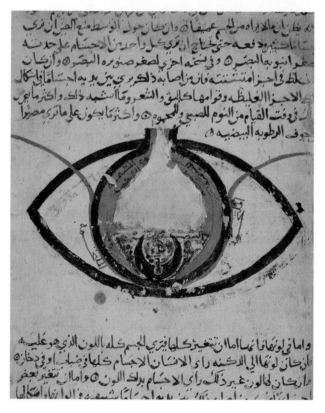

This 12th-century Arabic treatise on eye diseases is evidence of the detailed knowledge that some Muslim doctors had about the human body. Although Muslim physicians based much of their work on Greek and Indian science, they made major advances in the science of human anatomy.

for a hospital. Drawing on his many observations and experiences, ar-Razi compiled a multivolume encyclopedia of medical knowledge. His fellow Muslims did not always appreciate his work, however. When he offended another scholar, his rival ordered that he be beaten over the head with his book until one of them broke first. Unfortunately for Razi, it was his head that broke first, and as a result he went gradually blind.

Like many ancient Greek philosophers, the great Muslim philosopher Abu Raihan al-Biruni had broad interests, and he made contributions to a wide range of fields, including history, geography, medicine, chemistry, mathematics, and astronomy. He suggested that the Earth rotates on its axis. Al-Biruni even calculated the Earth's radius at about 3,867 miles (6,340 kilometers)—which is exactly right.

While the House of Wisdom in Baghdad was abuzz with intellectual activity, the western half of the Muslim empire developed its own centers of scholarship. In North Africa, Qayrawan and Fez became the main centers of Islamic thought, while in Spain, Seville and Cordoba became the primary centers of intellectual and cultural life.

A North African scholar named Abu Zayd ibn Khaldun was one of the first thinkers to develop a theory of how societies change. In his introduction to a long book on history and statesmanship, he thoroughly described the cycle that every civilization goes through, from birth, to greatness, to decline and disintegration. He was especially harsh in his assessment of the Bedouin's role in history. He wrote: "[Bedouin] dominate only of the plains, because they are, by their savage nature, people of pillage and corruption. They pillage everything that they can take without fighting or taking risks, then flee to their refuge in the wilderness, and do not stand and do battle unless in self-defense." His eastern counterparts in Baghdad probably debated this point.

Two Andalusian scholars would eventually make an enormous impact on European thinking. The logician Ibn Tufayl tried to show by way of a story that logic and reason can lead to the same truths as religion. In his book *Alive, Son of Awake,* Ibn Tufayl places the hero, a boy named Hayy,

The doe felt sorry for the infant and nuzzled him tenderly. She gave him her udder and let him drink her own delicious milk. She became his constant nurse, caring for him, raising him and protecting him from harm. . . .

When they went out to forage and came back to rest they were accompanied by a troop of deer that went along to graze and stayed the night near where they slept. Thus the child lived among the deer, imitating their calls so well that eventually his voice and theirs could hardly be distinguished. In the same way he imitated all the bird calls and animal cries he heard with amazing accuracy. . . . The animals were used to him and he was used to them, so they were not afraid of each other.

—Ibn Tufayl, *Alive, Son of Awake,* 12th century

on an island where he is reared by a gazelle. Hayy teaches himself philosophy and through it arrives at the same truths as taught in scriptures such as the Bible and the Quran.

Ibn Tufayl's friend Ibn Rushd spent most of his life in Seville and Cordoba, where he worked as a physician and as a judge in a Muslim law court in the service of several minor sultans. Westerners know him by the name Averroes. Ibn Rushd shared Ibn Tufayl's view that philosophy and religious revelation are both true paths to wisdom. However, unlike Ibn Tufayl, Ibn Rushd studied philosophy very deeply and had an especially thorough understanding of the Greek philosopher Aristotle. Ibn Rushd used logical explanations, rather than literary examples, to demonstrate that philosophy and religion supported each other. Loosely translated, his great book is called *The Harmony of Religion and Philosophy*.

Taken together, these Islamic thinkers bequeathed considerable intellectual gifts to the world. Much of al-Haitham's work on optics was later translated into Latin, and it influenced the work of such Western scientists as Johannes Kepler and Francis Bacon. Scholars eventually translated ar-Razi's encyclopedia into Latin too, and the encyclopedia became a standard reference for doctors in Europe centuries later.

Ibn Khaldun's still-controversial ideas about the rise and fall of societies foreshadowed the 19th-century German philosopher Karl Marx, among other

In his hometown of Cordoba, a statue of the philosopher Ibn Rushd, or Averroes, commemorates his influence on European thought.

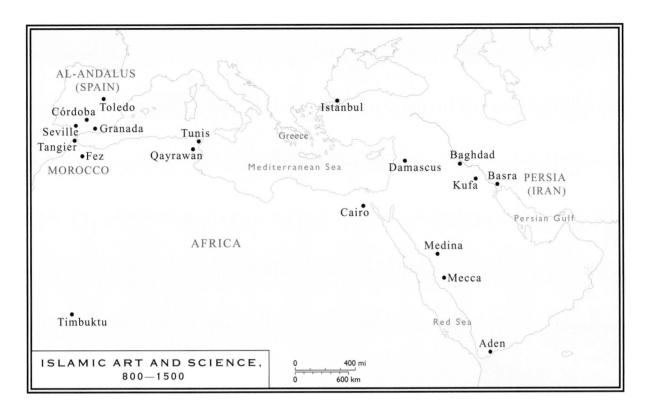

AL-ANDALUS
(SPAIN)

Córdoba • Toledo
Seville • Granada
Tangier
• Fez
MOROCCO

Tunis

Qayrawan

Istanbul

Greece

Mediterranean Sea

Cairo

AFRICA

Timbuktu

Damascus

Kufa

Baghdad

Basra PERSIA
(IRAN)

Persian Gulf

Medina

• Mecca

Red Sea

Aden

**ISLAMIC ART AND SCIENCE,
800—1500**

0   400 mi
0   600 km

modern writers and thinkers. Ibn Tufayl's *Alive* influenced the 18th-century British novelist Daniel Defoe as he wrote the great adventure tale of Robinson Crusoe, about an Englishman stranded on an island. Ibn Rushd's efforts to bring philosophical logic and religious faith into line with each other inspired medieval Christian thinkers such as Thomas Aquinas, who tried to use logic to demonstrate the truth of the Bible.

Another gift of the Islamic thinkers to the European world was their preservation of ancient Greek ideas. Through translations of Biruni, Ibn Rushd, and others, medieval Europeans rediscovered the work of ancient Greeks that had been lost to them since the fall of Rome in the 5th century. This introduction to ancient ideas, particularly Aristotle's observations about the natural world and how it worked, helped to kick off a revolution in thought in 14th-century Europe that would come to be known as the Renaissance.

"A BOOK OF VERSE——AND THOU": ISLAMIC ARTS AND LETTERS

Muslims, including Muhammad, were instructed by God to "Go in search of knowledge, even to China." The amateur geographer and observer of foreign cultures from Morocco, Abu Abdallah ibn Battuta, did just that. Ibn Battuta was born in Tangier around 1304. After he studied Islamic law in Moroccan schools, he left the city in 1325 on a voyage to see the world and to perform the pilgrimage to Islam's holy cities of Mecca and Medina. It was customary for Muslims from the western lands of Islam to travel as Ibn Battuta did so that they could learn firsthand from the birthplace of Islam. They called this journey a *rihla*, a voyage undertaken for religious and educational reasons. Its purpose was to "see the world" as God had created it in all its variety. Yet it is unlikely that anyone roamed the world as extensively as Ibn Battuta did.

Over the next 29 years, he visited Mecca and performed the pilgrimage a total of seven times. What's more, he trekked the entire length and breadth of the Islamic world from Spain to China, from southern Russia to the heart of Africa.

Ibn Battuta's first *rihla* lasted more than a quarter of a century, and when he finally returned home, he found that his father had died years before and that only days before, the bubonic plague had struck Tangier, killing his mother. Ibn Battuta soon grew restless and set off to visit Spain. Ibn Battuta found Toledo and Seville to be sunbathed, colorful places, much like his North African hometown. The gentle yellows, tans, browns, pinks, and reds of their brick and plaster buildings were heightened by brilliant colors from

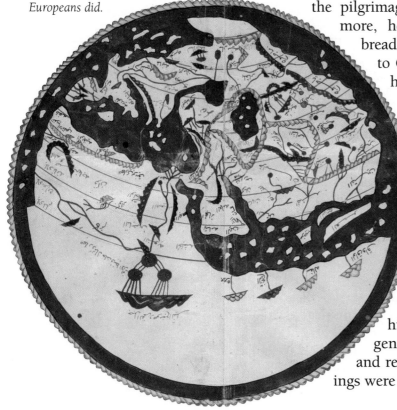

The 12th-century Muslim geographer al-Idrisi knew enough about the world to ink in Europe, the Mediterranean, North Africa, Arabia, the Red Sea, the Persian Gulf, the Indian Ocean, and even China on this map from his 1154 atlas. This is the world that was known to Ibn Battuta. By the 12th century, Muslim geographers and mapmakers knew much more about geography than Europeans did.

the flowers, fruits, and trees of the gardens, as well as the beautifully dyed clothing of the people who lived and moved about in them. People who lived in Islamic cities such as Tunis, Tangier, Toledo, and Seville enjoyed lovely gardens, public street lighting, sanitation, and sewage removal. (While this must all have seemed normal to Ibn Battuta, medieval European travelers from north of Spain, used to the foulness of their own cities, would have been astonished by such facilities.)

In the account of his travels, which he dictated afterwards to a secretary, Ibn Battuta describes visiting "the metropolis of Andalusia and the bride of its cities"—Granada:

The roof of the Great Mosque at Cordoba is supported by arcades of horseshoe-shaped arches, which themselves rest on a whole forest of carved marble columns.

continued on page 86

Don't Drink the Water

**"THE TALE OF KING SINDBAD AND THE FALCON,"
THE THOUSAND AND ONE NIGHTS, 10TH–14TH CENTURIES**

The Thousand and One Nights is an assortment of tall tales that Islamic storytellers collected over several centuries. Nobody knows for sure the exact date of any of the stories. Some seem to have originated as early as the 10th century, while others date from the later Middle Ages, perhaps as late as the 14th century. The yarns came from all over the Middle East and the lands that bordered the Indian Ocean. Although we don't know who the author or authors were, the tales often have a message about how to live one's life. In this sad story, King Sindbad learns not to judge too quickly.

They say that there was a king among the King of Fars who was a great lover of sport, of riding through the great gardens, and of all kinds of hunting. He had a falcon which he had trained himself and which never left him by day or night; for even during the night he carried it upon his fist and when he went hunting and coursing took it with him. He had also a little cup of gold hung from her neck at which she used to drink.

One day, as he was sitting in his palace, his chief falconer approached him, saying: "King of the ages, the weather is just right for hunting." The King made ready and, taking his falcon, set out with a great company and came at length to a valley where they spread the hunting nets. Suddenly a gazelle fell into the nets, and the King said: "I will kill him who lets her pass." Then they began to narrow the hunting net about the gazelle so that she came near the King and, standing on her hind legs, brought her forelegs close to her chest, as if she wished to salute him. On this the King clapped his hands to frighten the gazelle and she leapt over his head and fled far away over the plain.

Turning to his huntsmen, the King saw them winking at each other, so he asked his wazir [minister] why they were winking and the other answered: "I think they are reminding each other of what you said, that you would put anyone to death who let the gazelle pass." Then the King cried out: "By my life, we must follow this gazelle and bring her back!" So he galloped at full speed on her track, and when he came up to her, the falcon struck her above the eyes with his beak, blinding and bewildering her, and the King took his mace and rolled her over with one blow. Then he dismounted to disembowel and flay the animal, and afterwards hung the carcass on his saddle-bow.

By this time, both the King and his horse had become faint from thirst, the day being very hot and the place a dry waterless desert; but, chancing to look round, the King saw a tree, down whose trunk water was falling as thick as butter. The King, who had his hands covered with leather gloves, took the cup from the falcon's neck, filled it with this water and placed it before the bird. But the falcon hit the cup with his claw and knocked it over. Again, the King filled it and, still thinking that the bird was thirsty, placed it before him, but the falcon knocked it over a second time. Then the King became angry with the bird and, filling the cup a third time, held it out to his horse, but the falcon fluttered forward and knocked it over with his wing.

"Allah entomb you, you ill-omened bird!" cried the King. "You have prevented me from drinking and the horse also, to say nothing of your silly self!" So he struck at the falcon with his sword, and cut both her wings. Then the falcon lifted her head up, as if she were saying by signs, "Look into the tree!" The King looked up and saw in the tree a knot of serpents, dripping their venom-like water down the trunk. Seeing this, he was sorrowful for what he had done and, mounting his horse, rode back to his palace. Arrived there, he threw the carcass of the gazelle to the cook, telling him to prepare it. Then he sat down, still with the falcon on his hand: but no sooner had he done so than the bird gave a sob and fell dead. At this sight, the King uttered cries of lamentation and repentance that he had killed the bird who had saved him from a frightful death.

This is the tale of King Sindbad.

Middle Easterners had revered falcons since at least ancient Egyptian times.

continued from page 83

Its environs have not their equal in any country in the world. They extend for the space of forty miles, and are traversed by the celebrated river of [Xenil] and many other streams. Around it on every side are orchards, gardens, flowery meads, noble buildings, and vineyards. One of the most beautiful places there is "Ayn ad-dama" [the Fountain of Tears], which is a hill covered with gardens and orchards and has no parallel in any other country.

Without a doubt, the crowning achievement of Andalusian architecture and art was the 14th-century fortress in Granada called the Alhambra. The buildings appear unadorned on the outside, but, as with all Andalusian buildings, there is hidden beauty within the walls and turrets. The architects used columns extensively to provide support for ceilings and vaults plastered in complex geometric and floral designs. The center of the compound is a lovely courtyard called the Lion Court. Here a complex system of plumbing, operated entirely by gravity, allowed the flow of water into a central fountain, decorated with lions' heads. A testament to Islamic ingenuity, it still works to this day.

Ibn Battuta didn't restrict himself to buildings and gardens, however. Throughout his travels, he met people, both high and low, and recorded his impressions. In Granada,

[He was unable to meet the king] on account of an illness from which he was suffering, but the noble, pious, and virtuous woman, his mother, sent me some gold dinars, of which I made good use. I met at [Granada] a number of its distinguished scholars and the principal Shaykh, who is also the superior of the Sufi orders. I spent some days with him in his hermitage outside [Granada]. He showed me the greatest honour and went with me to visit the hospice, famed for its sanctity.

The Alhambra and its lush gardens are perhaps the most magnificent example of Islamic architecture that survived in Spain after the country was reconquered by Christians.

Ibn Battuta's 14th-century travelogue, translated as *Travels in Asia and Africa,* is one of the great contributions to world letters, and literature may in fact have been the greatest contribution of the Muslims to world art. The Abbasid court poets excelled at a form called *adab,* which combined earlier Persian rhyme schemes, words, and secular themes like love with Arabic to produce a literature that delighted the caliphs. But perhaps the best-known works to come out of this golden age were the tales collected as *The Thousand*

and One Nights and the poetry of the 11th-century Persian Omar Khayyám, who composed *The Rubaiyat.*

The Thousand and One Nights is a collection of hundreds of stories as told by the book's heroine, Shahrazad. Shahrazad's father has been forced to marry his beloved daughter to an evil king who kills a new wife every night. According to the first story,

> Shahrazad had read the books, the annals, and the legends of old kings, together with the histories of past peoples. Also she was credited with possessing a thousand books of stories telling of the peoples, the kings, and the poets of bygone ages and of past time. She was sweetly eloquent of speech and to listen to her was music.

Shahrazad saves herself by telling the king a series of never-ending cliffhangers about kings, *shaykhs,* ministers, doctors, fishermen, merchants, and many other characters in installments for hundreds of nights.

In his collection of verses called *The Rubaiyat,* the Sufi poet Omar Khayyám used sensual pleasures to represent the feeling of being near to God. In 1859, the Englishman Edward Fitzgerald freely translated the poem into English, and it became popular throughout Europe. In Fitzgerald's translation, Omar Khayyám basks in the glory of God through the symbols of food, wine, and poetry:

> Here with a Loaf of Bread beneath the Bough,
> A Flask of Wine, a Book of Verse—and Thou
> Beside me singing in the Wilderness—
> And Wilderness is Paradise enow [enough].

In North Africa and Al-Andalus, Muslims developed their own styles of poetry, different from Islamic verse in Arabia and Persia. Andalusians and North Africans favored words that were more worldly than the divinely inspired lyrics of the Middle East. Around the 10th century, Arabic verse styles blended with the Spanish language to produce an Andalusian form of poetry called the *zejel.* Often concerned with themes of love, these simple verses built from repeated lines reflect the earthiness of North African and Spanish Islamic culture. In one *zejel* entitled "Three Moorish Maidens Fair," an anonymous poet contemplates his crush on three North African girls who, much like himself, keep running out of luck. "Moor" is what the Europeans called Arabs and Berbers.

Three Moorish maidens enchanted me
in Ja-en [a Moorish town].
Aisha, Fatima, and Marien

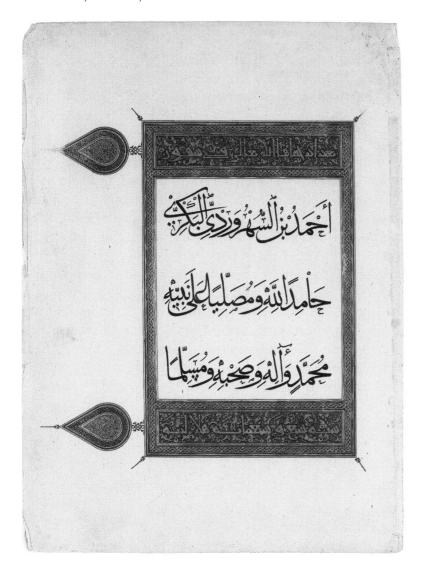

The Quran forbade artists to represent people, because that was considered to be idol worship. So, for many centuries, art took the forms of abstract geometric designs and written passages from the Muslim holy book executed in ornamental styles. This page comes from a 13th-century Quran.

Three Moorish maidens fair
Were going to pick olives,
[And] found the trees were bare
in Ja-en.
Aisha, Fatima, and Marien

The olives were all gone,
The little maids forlorn.
Their faces lost their bloom
in Ja-en.
Aisha, Fatima, and Marien

Three Moorish maidens so fair,
Three Moorish maidens so fair,
They went to pick some pears
in Ja-en.
Aisha, Fatima, and Marien

Although most of the Berbers of North Africa had converted to Islam soon after the Arabs arrived, in Spain most of the native population practiced Christianity or Judaism, which enjoyed a golden age in medieval Islamic Spain. With many Arabs and Berbers forming the ruling class, inevitably Islamic and Arab-Berber tastes and ways of life crept into Spanish civilization. Spanish Christians and Jews spoke and wrote in Arabic. Arab and Berber cultures also gave Spain the guitar and castanets. And flamenco dancing, with its spirited hand clapping, came from Arab and Berber forms and rhythms. You didn't have to believe that Muhammad was God's Prophet to enjoy the arts and ideas that Muslim rule brought to your town.

CHAPTER 8

NOW IT'S ISTANBUL, NOT CONSTANTINOPLE
THE OTTOMAN EMPIRE

For centuries Muslims had tried to defeat the Byzantines once and for all. By the 13th century, the once sprawling Byzantine Empire had shrunk to cover only eastern Anatolia and Europe's southern Balkan mountain range. But the last great defenders of Christendom against Islamic expansion in the eastern Mediterranean kept hanging tough. Time and time again, the Byzantines drove Muslim armies back from Anatolia and from the walls of their capital at Constantinople.

In 1071, the tide finally began to turn, when the Seljuk Turks defeated the Byzantines at the Battle of Manzikert, in northern Syria. According to a 10th-century historian,

> [T]he Turk will hit from his saddle an animal, a bird, a target, a man, a crouching animal, a marker post or a bird of prey stooping on its quarry. His horse may be exhausted from being galloped and reined in, wheeled to the right and left, and mounted and dismounted: but he himself goes on shooting, loosing ten arrows before [another] has let fly one.

With such single-minded determination, these warriors (ghazis in Turkish) relentlessly pursued the armies of Byzantium. Following their conquest at

Many Ottoman soldiers could shoot their curved bows at full gallop. Such skill enabled them to easily overcome the European, Persian, and Arab armies they faced in battle.

Curved bows made from horn and wood were the weapons of choice for the Turkish and Mongolian soldiers who conquered the Islamic world and then converted to Islam. Over the centuries, these bowmen learned to join wood, horn, and sinew in such a way that the tips "recurved" forward. Powerful and small, such bows were ideal for shooting at targets from horseback.

Manzikert, the Turks pushed into Anatolia (what we now call Turkey) and established what they called the Rum (Turkish for "Rome") sultanate in its eastern part.

The sultan of Rum appointed the leader of a band of Turkish warriors to govern a tiny province in western Anatolia. The governor's name was Osman. Osman's little province was a *ghazi* state, intended to protect the caliphate's borders from Christian attacks and expand Islamic sovereignty. But the Turks weren't the only game in town. In 1258, Hulegu's Mongol hordes took Baghdad from the Seljuk Turks, and around 1300, the Mongols completely destroyed the Rum sultanate. Freed from his obligations to the sultans, Osman seized the opportunity to conquer and expand his tiny *ghazi* state. A charismatic leader, Osman inspired his followers, who were eager to use their fighting skills to defeat the enemies of Islam.

Osman's sultanate was crudely organized. In fact, it had no real government at all. Osman was simply a chieftain who commanded a rough, often rebellious tribe of Turks. In many respects, his sultanate resembled Arabia before Muhammad. The only organization in this *ghazi* state was two religious brotherhoods, or *tariqas*, to which Osman and his mounted warriors belonged. Very likely, part of Osman's authority came from being a *tariqa* leader.

By the time he died in 1326, Osman's holdings had grown to include almost all of northwestern Anatolia. His budding sultanate had become the most powerful one among several in Anatolia, and soon it would flourish as the great Ottoman Empire. As he lay dying, Osman told his son to keep fighting, to take more lands, to "cultivate justice and thereby embellish the earth. Rejoice my departed soul with a beautiful series of victories . . . propagate religion by thy arms." His son, Orhan, did just that.

Orhan alternated his campaigns yearly between his Turkish neighbors to the east and the Byzantines to the west, steadily pushing the boundaries of his empire outward. "Of fortresses he possesses nearly a hundred, and for most of his time he is continually engaged in making the rounds of them," recorded the traveler Ibn Battuta, who had been welcomed at Orhan's court. "It is said that he has never stayed for a whole month in any town. He also fights with the infidels continually and keeps them under siege." (Infidels were the people who didn't believe in Islam.)

In time, Orhan's Ottoman army had taken over most of Anatolia. Only the Balkan Peninsula remained in Byzantine hands, and its leadership was disintegrating. When a dispute erupted between Prince John Comnenus, son of the dead king, and another contestant for the Byzantine throne, Comnenus invited Orhan to cross from Anatolia to the Balkan Peninsula to intervene on his behalf. The strategy worked—Comnenus won the throne. But now he had an even bigger problem. Once on the peninsula, Orhan and the Ottomans were there to stay.

Orhan used his position to launch a successful invasion of southeastern Europe. To govern his expanding territory,

"[He was the] greatest of the Kings of the Turkmen Kings, and the richest in wealth, lands and military forces."

—Ibn Battuta, description of Orhan, *Travels in Asia and Africa,* 14th century

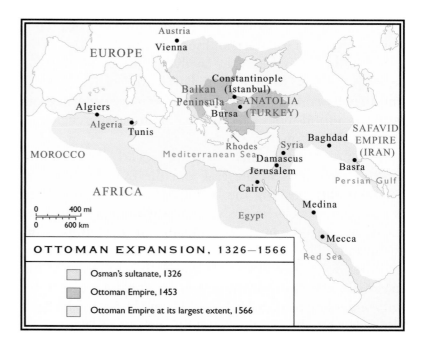

OTTOMAN EXPANSION, 1326–1566

- Osman's sultanate, 1326
- Ottoman Empire, 1453
- Ottoman Empire at its largest extent, 1566

Orhan transformed his father's loose alliance of tribal warriors into a more organized state. Osman's sultanate didn't even have a capital, but Orhan chose Bursa, Anatolia, as the center of his government. He also reorganized the army. In return for a promise of military service, Orhan gave each commander of mounted warriors his own estate. The system worked: it encouraged loyalty among the sultan's mounted cavalry.

CANNONS RULE THE DAY

The Ottomans were ruthless in their takeover of the Balkan Peninsula. In two 14th-century victories over Christian forces, they massacred all prisoners taken in battle. To make matters worse for their Christian subjects, between 1421 and 1451 Sultan Murad II introduced something called the *devshirme* ("harvest" of boys) system among Christian villagers in the Balkan Mountains. Every year, the sultan's officials went into these villages and selected the strongest and smartest boys. The children were taken away from their parents and into the capital, where they were forced to convert to Islam and then given the very best education. The Ottomans trained them in the arts of war, in addition to Islamic literature, law, and religious studies. Students were not allowed to leave the palace during their period of training. Eventually, some rose to the highest ranks in the sultan's administration.

Other *devshirme* boys trained for a new corps of foot soldiers, or infantry, called the Janissaries, or "New Troops." These infantrymen were the elite forces, and they soon gained a reputation as crack troops who led the Ottoman armies into battle. Equipped with the most advanced weapon of the day—guns—they were able to overcome any resistance. No other armies in the world were yet using guns and cannons, which the Turks cast for themselves. With conquest after gunpowder conquest in the Balkans and Anatolia, the Ottoman Empire grew rapidly.

In 1451, still hardly more than a boy, the sultan Mehmed came to the throne. At this point, the one prize that remained in Byzantine hands, the one place that had frustrated Muslim armies for centuries, was the great city of Constantinople. Despite his youth, Mehmed was determined to take it. His preparations took more than a year, during which he amassed an army of more than 200,000 men, in addition to the Janissaries and their fearsome cannons.

Rows of animals within animals make a clever pattern in this 14th-century Turkish carpet. Using Persian carpets as their models, Ottoman craftsmen learned to weave their own with a high degree of skill.

For centuries, Constantinople's mighty stone walls had defied all takers. However, in 1453, the Ottomans had another new weapon on their side. Traditional cannons were built from pieces of wood bound by metal strips. They were too weak to blast through the high walls of Constantinople. Ottoman inventors advanced the technology by casting cannons from brass or bronze. These metal cannons were much sturdier, and with them Ottoman gunners easily blew apart the stone walls of Constantinople.

When Mehmed "saw . . . the wall that had been destroyed . . . now empty of men and deserted by the defenders," he shouted to his soldiers to press on:

> Friends, we have the City! We have it! They are already fleeing from us! They can't stand it any longer! The wall is bare of defenders! It needs just a little more effort and the city is taken! Don't weaken, but on with the work with all your might, and be men and I am with you!

Although the author of this account, a Greek governor for the Ottomans named Kritovoulos, was not himself an eyewitness to the siege, he most likely relied on firsthand information for this story.

A fresco on the wall of a Romanian church marks the fall of Constantinople to Mehmed's troops in 1453. After the siege, Constantinople was renamed Istanbul and became the seat of the Ottoman Empire.

Kritovoulos continues to describe the sultan and his men:

[They were] pressing on up to the palisade. After a long and bitter struggle, they hurled back the [Byzantine defenders] from there and climbed by force up the palisade. They dashed some of their foe down into the ditch between the great wall and palisade, which was deep and hard to get out of, and they killed them there. The rest they drove back to the gate.

At the gate, the emperor, and "all who were with him, fell in gallant combat." Many of Constantinople's population fled or were killed.

Mehmed renamed the conquered city Istanbul and made it the capital of the Ottoman world. He converted the great Cathedral of Hagia Sophia, built in the 6th century by the Byzantine emperor Justinian, into a mosque.

SULEYMAN, HOW MAGNIFICENT!

Although Muslim rulers had long dreamed of adding Constantinople to their empire, they did not stop there. The Ottoman Empire reached its greatest size during the reign of Suleyman I, or Suleyman the Magnificent, in the 16th century. The sultan before him, Selim I, had defeated the Egyptians and added Egypt as an Ottoman province in 1516. When the young Suleyman came to the throne in 1520, the Spanish and the Portuguese had been attacking and occupying port cities of Morocco and Algeria for many years. Suleyman saw a chance to extend Ottoman holdings in Egypt farther across North Africa. He formed an alliance with a pirate-chief named Khair ad-Din Barbarossa, who used Algiers as his home port to raid Christian trading vessels on the Mediterranean. Together Khair ad-Din's experienced seamen and the well-armed Ottoman fleet pushed the Europeans out of Tunis and Algiers.

For many centuries, a brotherhood of Christian warriors called the Knights of Saint John had defended the Mediterranean island of Rhodes against the Ottomans. Just off the Anatolian coast, the Knights posed an immediate European threat to its Ottoman sultans. Suleyman laid siege to the island and finally forced the Knights to surrender. The Europeans were left with no foothold anywhere in the eastern Mediterranean. With these two successes in North Africa and Rhodes, Suleyman won control over most of the lands bordering the Mediterranean, not to mention the sea's trade and shipping.

Suleyman's next and boldest move was against the capital of the Austrian Empire, Vienna. After besieging the city through the summer in 1529, the onset of autumn and colder weather forced Suleyman to withdraw. Though this attack failed, it marked the crest of a long wave of Ottoman expansion in Europe.

Besides his attacks on Islamic North Africa and Christian Europe, Suleyman waged battles with a powerful Shiite state in Iran (the Safavids) and seized control of Baghdad and Basra from Shiite forces. It was at this time that Persia (now called Iran) was declared officially Shiite, as distinguished from Sunni Ottoman lands. During the reigns of Suleyman and his predecessors, the Sunni Islamic community had come to regard the Ottoman sultans as their leaders. Like his ancestors, Suleyman built mosques and schools, supported the work of the religious scholars, and gave them government jobs. In the spirit of the great caliphs before him, Suleyman organized religious education and the enforcement of Islamic law throughout the empire. He assembled the *ulama* into an elaborate chain of command, with a *shaykh al-Islam,* or head *shaykh* of religious matters, in charge.

Suleyman and his successors also arranged for annual pilgrimages to Mecca. Caravans of pilgrims gathered every year at Cairo and Damascus, where the sultan provided armed escorts to protect them from Bedouin bandits. At Mecca, the sultan's government put up tents and kitchens to house and feed the pilgrims and prepared a new covering for the Ka'ba. Suleyman also saw to it that the Tomb of the Prophet Muhammad in Medina and the Dome of the Rock mosque in Jerusalem were kept in good repair.

He built and maintained mosques throughout the empire, and he employed the architect Sinan Pasha to build hundreds of buildings in Istanbul. One result was the Suleymaniyya Mosque, completed in 1557. A magnificent dome, 172 feet high and 88 feet across, soared across the top, and needle-like towers around it rose gracefully into the sky. Mosque chanters (called muezzins) climbed these towers five times a day to call the faithful to prayer. Later architects imitated these features in their design of other Turkish mosques. Besides serving as a place for prayer, the Suleymaniyya Mosque included a school and a hospital.

Suleyman's empire was equally magnificent. But it seems that even a ruler as powerful as Suleyman could not escape the common problems of family life. He lived, like all the sultans did, in Istanbul's sprawling Topkapi Palace. Most of the Topkapi was for formal state functions. The private quarters, the place where the sultans' many wives, slaves, and children lived, was called the harem.

Suleyman's harem included a slave named Roxelana, whom the sultan liked so much that he made her a wife. Of course, each wife wanted to see her own son succeed as the next sultan, and Roxelana was no different. She was terribly jealous of Mustapha, Suleyman's favorite son by another wife and designated heir. She also

Eight pillars arranged around a massive square room and four half domes at the corners of the square help support the massive central dome of the Ottoman Selimiye Mosque. Such masterpieces earned Sinan Pasha, the greatest architect of Suleyman's reign, the nickname "Sinan the Great."

envied the power exercised by Suleyman's grand vizier (prime minister), who was his best friend.

Roxelana not only pressured Suleyman to remove the vizier, she hired an assassin to murder him once he had lost his position. Next, Roxelana convinced Suleyman that Mustapha was plotting to overthrow him. Fearful of mutiny, the sultan strangled his son. A European ambassador to Suleyman's court later reported, "Even his bitterest critics can find nothing more serious to allege against him than his undue submission to his wife [Roxelana] and its result in his somewhat [hasty] action in putting Mustapha . . . to death, which is generally [blamed on Roxelana's] employment of love potions and incantations."

The loss of both his best friend and well-loved son made Suleyman very sad. The ambassador wrote, "His expression . . . is anything but smiling, and has a sternness which,

The sprawling Topkapi Palace was home to the sultans for many centuries. Mehmed II had it built in 1465, just 12 years after he conquered Constantinople, and it remained the sultans' home until 1853.

The Great Sultan's Painted Face

AMBASSADOR OGIER GHISELIN DE BUSBECQ, LETTERS, 1554–1562

Near the end of the sultan's life, in 1561, a European ambassador named Ogier Ghiselin de Busbecq visited Suleyman's court. Sent by the emperor of the Hapsburg Empire, Busbecq got a rare glimpse into the personal life of the sultan, which he included in his report.

An Ottoman miniaturist painted this portrait of Suleyman the Magnificent as an old man one year before the European ambassador Ogier Ghiselin de Busbecq visited him. The aging sultan is followed by two dignitaries.

The Sultan was seated on a rather low sofa, no more than a foot from the ground and spread with many costly coverlets and cushions embroidered with exquisite work. Near him were his bows and arrows. . . .

He is beginning to feel the weight of years, but his dignity of demeanor and his general physical appearance are worthy of the ruler of so vast an empire. . . . Even in his earlier years he did not indulge in wine or in those unnatural vices to which the Turks are often addicted. . . . He is a strict guardian of his religion and its ceremonies. . . . For his age—he has almost reached his sixtieth year—he enjoys quite good health, though his bad complexion may be due to some hidden malady; and indeed it is generally believed that he has an incurable ulcer or gangrene on his leg. The defect of complexion he remedies by painting his face with a coating of red powder.

The various special troops in their victory oriented army and the various tools of war and battle . . . given to them were not available to the brawny fists of [previous kings]. To their attacks going downward and going upward are the same. . . . In their eyes the conquest of a castle is like destroying a spider's web, and in their God-assisted hands to beat the enemies is clearly like pulling out a hair from the beard of a decrepit old man.

—Mustafa Ali,
Counsel for Sultans,
1581

though sad is full of majesty." After Mustapha died, Suleyman showed less and less interest in administering his great empire and gradually withdrew from public life. Even in a dynasty that had many long-reigning sultans, Suleyman's rule had been a remarkably long and stable one. It had lasted for nearly half a century, from 1520 to 1566.

The Ottoman Empire was the last of the great Muslim empires. Following the reign of the mighty Suleyman, after more than 900 years of steady advances against Christian Europe, Muslims—the Ottomans in particular—began to suffer defeats and lose territory. Probably with some nostalgia for their golden age, a late-16th-century court official named Mustafa Ali wrote a book called *Counsel for Sultans,* in which he described the qualities that had made the earlier rulers so successful. He almost surely had Suleyman in mind when he wrote: "Their religious convictions being immaculate and their character like a shining mirror, it has never happened that a single member of that noble family [the Ottomans] ever swerved from the road of orthodoxy or that one valiant sultan befriended himself with an unseemly [religious] doctrine."

Despite Ali's *Counsel,* the sultans never rose again. By the 19th century, the Ottoman Empire had declined so far in military strength and wealth that Europeans called it "the sick man of Europe." Long gone were the glories of Harun al-Rashid of Baghdad and the days of Suleyman the Magnificent. The sultans managed to hold on to power until revolutionaries forced the last of them, Sultan Abdulhemid II, off his throne in 1907. The empire went down to its last great defeat in World War I, and in 1922 it became the modern nation of Turkey.

CHAPTER 9

WHERE GOLD GROWS AS CARROTS DO

GHANA AND THE AFRICAN GRASSLANDS

Just south of the Sahara Desert where the Berbers lived is a region called the Sahel, which receives a little rain. Some short grasses grow there. Across the Sahel, the landscape gradually changes from desert to grassland. In the vast African grasslands, people hunted wild game, such as antelope and monkeys, fished the rivers and lakes, and gathered plants, such as wild rice and other grains.

People of the grasslands lived in small villages and sometimes even towns. Their houses were small and usually circular, made from wood and packed mud, with cone-shaped roofs made of thatch. Their lives were hard. As farmers all over the world still do, they got out of bed before sunup. They'd start the day with an early meal of porridge

The Sahel Desert is too dry for growing crops, so villagers rely on livestock for their livelihoods.

This king of Awdaghost maintains relations with the ruler of Ghana. Ghana is the wealthiest king on the face of the earth because of his treasures and stocks of gold extracted in olden times for his predecessors and himself. He sends gifts to the ruler of Kugha (although Kugha does not approach the ruler of Ghana in opulence and well-being) and they send gifts to him. They stand in pressing need of [the goodwill of] the kings of Awdaghost because of the salt which comes to them from the lands of Islam. They cannot do without this salt, of which one load, in the interior and more remote parts of the land of the Sudan, may fetch between 200 and 300 dinars.

—Abu al-Qasim Muhammad Ibn Hawqal, description of the Berbers of the Maghrib, 10th century

or a thin gruel made out of boiled millet or sorghum—grains that make a dish like soupy oatmeal. According to one African story,

> [A]s God fashioned the first man, he thought again, "The man must be able to cultivate his millet, so I will give him two arms, one to hold the hoe, and the other to tear up the weeds." Later still, he thought again, "The man must be able to see his millet, so I will give him two eyes." Still not done, God thought, "The man must be able to eat his millet, so I will give him a mouth."

After breakfast, the men and boys would go off to herd livestock or hunt for wild game, while the women and girls went to the fields to tend to their farms. It was the men's job to clear the fields for planting and usually the women's job to plant, weed, water, and harvest. Old women and young girls stayed nearer to home to look after the small children. There was a lot of work to do around the house: milk pails to be cleaned, houses to be mended with new layers of mud and thatching, goats to be milked, and meals to be prepared. Some people also remained in the village to work in crafts, such as basket weaving, pottery making, or ironworking.

CARAVANS AND KINGDOMS: TRADE GIVES RISE TO GHANA

Some towns thrived by trading gold, slaves, and kola nuts (the narcotic seed of an African plant) for dates, copper, horses, cloth, and weapons that the Berbers brought from the oases of the desert and from North Africa. Caravans coming from northern towns frequently stopped at oases near natural salt deposits to obtain salt, as well as luxuries like dates, which they transported south to trade with people of the borderlands and grasslands. West Africans were especially keen to trade for salt, which they used to preserve their food in the hot climate, not to mention make it taste good.

A caravan could number as many as 3,000 camels and other livestock, along with hundreds of people. Merchants loaded up their camels with tons of dates, salt, copper, tin, gold (going north), and manufactured goods such as finely crafted swords, shields, ivory, textiles, leather goods, books, and jewelry. Besides the merchants, among the people were their slaves, Berber guides and hired guards, travelers, and bound slaves, seized mostly from the forest people, headed for North Africa. Except perhaps for the family members traveling with the Berbers and female slaves, there wouldn't have been many women.

The dangerous journey across the burning sand and rocks of the desert took as many as four months to complete. The caravans traveled slowly from water hole to water hole, traveling in the early hours of the day and in the evening hours, but stopping to rest and take shelter where they could in the heat of midday. Occasionally, caravans got lost in the vastness of the Sahara, and when that happened, everyone perished from heat exhaustion, thirst, and dehydration. So when a caravan made it safely to its destination, there'd be a big celebration, with music and everyone dancing and feasting on roasted goats and couscous, a Berber dish made from semolina (the wheat flour that's used for making pasta), topped with spicy stewed meat and vegetables.

Rock paintings throughout the Sahara Desert show galloping horses pulling people in chariots. From such ancient artwork, scholars have concluded that people traveled for short distances, possibly for trade, using horse-drawn vehicles. The camel was not introduced into the western Sahara until the 4th century.

All of this trade brought tremendous wealth to the towns, so much that some towns grew into cities, and some cities grew into kingdoms. Nestled between the Senegal and Niger Rivers, Ghana was just such a kingdom. The Niger River in West Africa arches into the desert borderlands. Besides being an important source of fish, it has served as a

Berber and West African women adorned themselves with heavy bracelets such as these made from gold, silver, and coral.

major highway of boat transportation and trade for centuries. Ghana was in the perfect spot for taking advantage of the gold trade. The capital at Kumbi Saleh was located almost exactly midway between the gold fields at Bambuk near the Senegal River and the saltworks to the north. Ghana earned a reputation as being the land where gold was most abundant.

Many North African travelers and merchants thought that in Ghana gold simply grew out of the ground. In the 10th century, a Muslim geographer wrote, "In the country of Ghana gold grows in the sand as carrots do, and

Ghana imported salt from desert oases such as Taghaza and shipped it south. In turn, Ghana merchants sold the salt to Bambuk for gold. The buyers carried the gold to Ghana, where they exchanged it with Arab and Berber merchants who shipped it to the major North African commercial cities such as Sijilmasa and Zawila.

is plucked at sunrise." As a matter of fact, this was far from the truth. Most of the people who dug for gold made their living primarily as farmers. They mined gold only when they wanted to have something to trade for goods they didn't have, such as salt or cloth.

Around 400, various small chiefdoms of a people called Soninke had united under the rule of a single king, whom they called the "Ghana." (The kingdom took its name from this word.) Very likely the Ghana was a divine king. Divine kings were as common in Africa as they were in ancient Egypt. Everyone believed that the king had sacred powers, and the Soninke often thought that a powerful spirit possessed him.

The Soninke people considered the Ghana's health to be crucial to the "health" of their land and his subjects. Most Africans believed in an all-powerful God who created the world. They also believed in many lesser gods and spirits, including the spirits of nature and the dead. These gods and spirits controlled the forces of nature, so it made sense to perform regular rituals and make sacrifices to these spirits to avoid disasters such as sickness, crop failures, droughts, insect infestations, and death. In places like Ghana where the king was considered divine, the king performed the rituals and made the sacrifices that were considered essential to the welfare of the entire land, especially its farmers. The Ghana found himself constantly sacrificing some small animal to one god or spirit or another. The point of all this special treatment was to keep the spirits happy so that they would bring much-needed rain and fertility to the land, the livestock, and the people.

If you were the Ghana, you would have inherited the job from your mother's brother. Sometimes you couldn't let anybody see you eating or sleeping—only "humans" needed to do that. Your feet were not allowed to touch the bare ground, and you'd meet your ministers, subjects, and visitors to court on raised platforms under giant umbrellas. You'd wear a fine silk cloak and trousers, a turban, and slippers that were unlike anyone else's. Though he'd never actually met one, a wealthy 11th-century Spanish Muslim

I saw one of their tribe who wished to capture one of some camels which had been alarmed. He posted himself in the path of these frightened runaway camels—who were all prime stallions—and seized the narrow part of its leg while it was in full flight, for he was running at the same speed. Then he prevented it from moving until he threw it to the ground and cut its throat as though he were merely slaughtering a goat or breaking [the neck of] a kid.

—Abu l-Qasim Muhammad Ibn Hawqal, description of the Berbers of the Maghrib, 10th century named Abu Ubayd 'Abd Allah al-Bakri described the Ghana based on other people's accounts: "The king adorns himself like a woman [wearing necklaces] round his neck and bracelets on his forearms, and he puts on a high cap . . . decorated with gold and wrapped in a turban of fine cotton." Trumpets and drums announced your arrival wherever you went, and people approached you on their bellies, sprinkling dust on their heads.

You have many court officials, and all territorial chiefs derive their own powers directly from you. Still, governing Ghana is a big job, so you have a council to help you—the council is made up of your mother and probably a court historian, a commander of the army, and territorial chiefs and officials. Like the king described by al-Bakri, you hold court

> in a domed pavilion around which stand ten horses covered with gold-embroidered materials. Behind the king stand ten pages holding shields and swords decorated with gold, and on his right are the sons of the [vassal] kings of his country wearing splendid garments and their hair plaited with gold. The governor of the city sits on the ground before the king and around him are ministers seated likewise.

In this 19th-century photograph from Africa, slaves carry their king and shield him with an umbrella, as court officials follow. In earlier centuries, divine kings of Ghana received similar kinds of royal treatment.

"At the door of the pavilion are dogs of excellent pedigree who hardly ever leave the place where the king is, guarding him. Round their necks they wear collars of gold and silver studded with a number of balls of the same metals."

—Spanish historian Abdul-Aziz al-Bakri,
description of the court of the Ghanian king
in *Lords and Kingdoms*, 1067

Still, surrounded by all this pomp, you couldn't get too cocky, because your mother had the power to veto your decisions.

One of your duties is to sort out conflict within your kingdom. To be remembered as a good king, you'll have to bring peace along with prosperity, which means you have to judge wisely and take charge when complaints are brought before you. You are the judge of final appeal, and once you pass judgment, you have to make sure your decisions are carried out.

WEST AFRICA FINDS ALLAH— AND LEARNS A NEW LANGUAGE

Along with salt, the Berbers brought the religion of Islam. As early as the 8th century, the first Muslims in West Africa were North African merchants living in the great trading cities. Few Africans in this area of the Sudan (the name for the West African grasslands) were converted as early as the 8th century, however. Islam remained, for a while at least, mostly limited to "foreigners" from the north and to Berber desert oases and the merchants' quarters of the cities.

Al-Bakri described Kumbi Saleh as "two towns situated on a plain." One was for the Muslim merchants. According

Two playful elephants represent their species in The Benefits of Animals, *a book by the 13th-century Persian geographer Ibn Bakhtishu. Middle Eastern geographers knew enough about African animals to portray them with considerable accuracy.*

Sanhaja are divided into 70 tribes. . . . In each confederation and tribe there are clans, lineages, and [sub-]tribes more numerous than can be numerated. All these tribes are desert-dwellers. Their territory is in the South, and extends for a distance of seven months long and four months wide, . . .

—Ibn Abi Zar, in his history of Morocco, around 1326

to al-Bakri, this town, "which is inhabited by Muslims, is large and possesses twelve mosques. . . . There are salaried imams [prayer leaders] . . . as well as jurists and scholars." The other town was for the unconverted king and the priests of the traditional African religion practiced by the king and his Soninke subjects: "The king's town is six miles distant from this one. . . . Around the king's town are domed buildings and groves and thickets where the sorcerers of these people, men in charge of the religious cult, live. In them too are their idols and the tombs of their kings."

The Ghana described in al-Bakri's account was not a Muslim. However, al-Bakri wrote, "The king's interpreters, the official in charge of his treasury and the majority of his ministers are Muslims." The Ghana surrounded himself with Muslim advisers, who brought their precious skills of reading and writing, as well as their knowledge of accounting and the written Islamic law. Written Islamic law had to be in Arabic, so wherever Islam went, the Arabic language did too.

In one of his many books on geography and religion, al-Bakri described the rituals of the king Tunka Manin and his court:

> The audience is announced by the beating of a drum which they call duba, made from a long hollow log. When the people who profess the same religion as the king approach him they fall on their knees and sprinkle dust on their heads, for this is their way of greeting him. As for the Muslims, they greet him only by clapping their hands.

All this changed in the 11th century. In 1036, a scholar named Abdallah ibn Yasin from the Muslim university in the Tunisian city of Qayrawan arrived among the Sanhaja Berbers of the western Sahara to enforce greater obedience to strict Sunni Islamic principles. When many refused, he established a *ribat*, a center of religious study similar to a monastery. A story by a North African historian tells how Abdallah ibn Yasin began preaching to the Berber tribesmen:

> [He] stayed with his companions worshipping God for three months. People heard about them from each other [and that] they sought Paradise and deliverance from Hellfire, and so the number of those who came to visit them and those who had repented increased. 'Abdallah bin Yasin began to preach them the Quran, to win them over to what was good.

Cordoban craftsmen carved hundreds of thousands of pieces of wood and bone and fit them all together to build this wooden pulpit. Installed at a Moroccan mosque, it stands about 13 feet tall.

It's Good to Have a Rich Sister

MUHAMMAD IBN HAWQAL, DESCRIPTION OF THE WORLD, 980

A fierce sense of independence characterized the Berbers of North Africa—and they were equally fierce in waging war to fight to keep their freedom. In this 10th-century account, the geographer and traveler ibn Hawqal describes a defensive Sanhaja Berber attack on another tribe.

[O]nce a certain Berber tribe went in great numbers and well-armed to the region of [the Sanhaja king]. . . . They were seeking an opportunity to catch them unawares on account of a grudge which they bore towards certain of the Sanhaja. Timbarutan, the king of the Sanhaja, heard of this and was reminded several times of their situation, and their intention in being on the road. He made no comment on it, but unknown to anyone summoned the herdsmen of his sister, who was the richest person of her tribe, owning the most livestock, and said to them: "You are near to such-and-such a watering place, and the Banu So-and-So will reach your area on such-and-such a night. At first dawn after that night you must rouse all the camels that are there on such-and-such a hill and stampede them on the enemy. Keep secret what I am telling you so that you may receive recompense from me, if God wills."

The enemy came and encamped and the herdsmen stampeded the camels, directing them towards the place and the enemy with their camels and arms, by trampling them underfoot. The news spread among all the people in Awdaghost and among their enemies dwelling far away that there was absolutely no recognizable trace left of them or their possessions, and they were utterly dispersed. The king's sister's herdsmen numbered a hundred, and each herdsman had 150 camels. In the morning they came to the king in order to congratulate him. Thus did God requite the deeds of the evildoers.

Construction began on the Great Mosque at Qayrawan in 670, making it one of the oldest Islamic buildings in North Africa. The courtyard, built in the 9th century, became a major center for teaching Islamic law.

Ribats like Abdallah ibn Yasin's helped to spread Islam and Arabic from coastal cities such as Qayrawan and Fez into the remote regions of the Sahara Desert. However, they were not convincing enough to convert the Sanhaja Berbers or the West Africans. Because they identified any form of Sunni Islam with their Arab rulers, many Berbers rejected ibn Yasin and the *ribats* and clung to Kharijism or Shiism, the two minority forms of Islam. Ibn Yasin finally resorted to force and declared a jihad (holy war) to force them to abandon their heretical beliefs. He and his armed followers were called the Almoravids or, in Arabic, the Al-Murabitun, which means "the men of the *ribat.*" Abdallah was killed, but the jihad continued to spread into parts of West Africa, as well as north into North Africa and Spain by 1090. The Almoravid jihad stamped out Shiite and Kharijite Islam, and Sunni Islam became the accepted form of Islam all over both North and West Africa after the 11th century.

During these Islamic holy wars, the Almoravids seized the Sanhaja caravan center, called Awdaghost, and fought against Ghana, as well as other Sudanese kingdoms, to convert the Sudanese to Islam by force. This jihad was not nearly as successful in West Africa as it was to the north, but it contributed to Ghana's decline. By the 12th century, the kings of Ghana had converted to Islam, and their kingdom broke apart. The warlike Berbers forced many of the Soninke people of Ghana to migrate southward, away from their native grasslands and closer to the West African forests.

They are a people who do not know of ploughing, sowing, or produce; their property consists only of camels and they live on flesh and milk. One of them may pass his life without eating bread unless merchants happen to pass through their country and give them some bread or flour as a gift.

—Ibn Abi Zar, describing Sanhaja Berbers in his history of Morocco, around 1326

CHAPTER 10

SADDLEBAGS STUFFED WITH GOLD
THE EMPIRES OF MALI AND SONGHAY

As Ghana's empire collapsed, a new Soninke kingdom called the Sosso rose to power. Around 1235, a powerful chief of an African people called the Mandinka came along to challenge their leader, Sumanguru. The Mandinka chief was a man named Sundiata. Sundiata united all the Mandinka-speaking chiefdoms into an alliance and led a Mandinka army against the Sosso. Modern historians know the story of the battle because it's been passed down through generations of African poet-historians called griots. The griots say, "In all these villages Sundiata recruited soldiers. In the same way as light precedes the sun, so the glory of Sundiata, overleaping the mountains, shed itself on all the Niger plain." From the praising language in this quote, you can probably tell who won the battle.

The Sosso lost, and within just a few years, Sundiata carved out a large empire for himself that included much of the western Sudan, including old Ghana. The new empire was named Mali.

In the mid-Senegal River region, the old gold diggings at Bambuk that had made Ghana wealthy had begun to run

"As for Sundiata, he defeated the army of Sumanguru, ravaged the land of the Sosso and subjugated its people. Afterwards Sundiata became the ruler of an immense empire."

—Anonymous Arabic manuscript

The Niger River was as important to the kingdoms of Mali and Songhay as the Nile was to the ancient Egyptians. Farmers relied on it for water and minerals for their fields and merchants depended on it to transport their gold and other goods. The city of Mopti still survives as a center of Niger commerce, much like those of long ago.

out. But lucky miners found huge new sources elsewhere. The first place where they struck gold was in the region of Buré, and Sundiata had his capital, Niani, near there. Buré was farther south than Bambuk, around the headwaters of the Niger River, which would be necessary for trading and transporting the gold. In the 14th century, miners found gold again, at a place called Bitu, just north of the rain forest and east of the Volta River. These two discoveries gave an enormous boost to the West African gold trade.

"Jenne is one of the great markets of the Muslim world," wrote the 17th-century historian from Timbuktu, Abd al-Rahman ibn Abdallah al-Sadi. Located on the Niger River and near the southern gold mines, the city of Jenne reaped huge benefits from this new trade. As al-Sadi explained,

MALI AND SONGHAY, 1200—1590

Mali   Songhay   Gold field

Merchants bring salt from the mines of Taghaza [a desert oasis] and those with gold from the mines of Bitu meet [at Jenne]. These two marvelous mines have no equal in the entire universe. Everyone going to Jenne to trade reaps large profits and thus acquires fortunes whose amount can be known only to God. (May he be praised!) Because of this city, caravans flock to Timbuktu from all points of the horizon.

Downriver from Jenne, the city of Timbuktu became the central trans-Saharan caravan port by the 14th century. Sundiata's successors enlarged the Mali Empire to include Jenne, Timbuktu, and another bustling trading city of the Niger River, Gao. Mali extended all the way to the Atlantic coast and was even bigger than Ghana had been.

MUSLIMS SPEAKING MANDINKA

By the 13th century, most of the gold circulating in North Africa and Europe came from the western Sudan. The gold trade brought traders to Africa in droves, many of whom were Arab Muslims. By the 14th century, nearly all of the ruling clans of the western Sudan had adopted the religion that these traders brought. But most of the Mandinka people were farmers, and the farmers continued to practice their traditional religion, which emphasized beliefs in nature spirits and gods who brought rainfall and made the land fertile. More than gold, Mali's prosperity depended on agriculture, and agriculture, to the Mandinka, depended on happy gods and spirits. The Mandinka kings, called *mansas,* may all have been Muslims, but the farmers gave them permission to rule based on their special status as "owners of the soil" and their connections to the Mandinka gods and spirits. People in Africa who claimed to be the oldest settlers in a certain place called themselves the "owners of the soil" because they claim their ancestors were the first to be buried there. They believed the spirits of these dead ancestors continued to inhabit the land and exercised a lot of power over it and the things they grew on it. So they thought that it was essential to pray to these spirits and make frequent offerings of small bits of grain and meat to make the spirits happy.

Like the Ghana before them, the *mansas* combined both kingly and religious powers. Alongside their worship of God, the earliest *mansas* continued to serve as the guardians of their royal ancestors. Since rainfall and fertility were

"Through these lands flows a very large river, which at certain times of the year floods all these lands. . . . There are many boats on it, by which they carry on trade."

—An Italian merchant, letter in which he describes the Niger River, 1447

essential to Mandinka survival, the *mansas* had to continue some traditional Sudanese practices, such as animal sacrifice and other rituals. After the 14th century, kings such as Mansa Musa tried to be more faithful to the teachings of Islam. Around 1324, Mansa Musa made an extravagant pilgrimage to Mecca, traveling with a caravan of camels whose saddlebags were stuffed with gold. One of the men who went with Mansa Musa on his pilgrimage later described it to the historian Ibn Khaldun, who recorded this firsthand account of luxurious travel: "We used to keep the Sultan company during his progress . . . and converse to his enjoyment. At each halt, he would regale us with rare foods and confectionery. His equipment and furnishings were carried by 12,000 private slave women, wearing gowns of brocade and Yemeni silk."

Mansa Musa made presents of gold to the sultans and various dignitaries he met along the way. His extraordinary pilgrimage spread his fame not only in the lands of Islam but in Europe as well. When an artist from Europe made a map of Mali a few decades later, he included a picture of Mansa Musa with a golden orb, a European symbol of royalty. Musa's reputation long outlived him, and several historians recorded that he gave away so much gold that for a long time afterwards the commercial value of gold was greatly reduced.

By the time of Musa's successor, Mansa Sulayman, in 1341, Mali was at its wealthiest, largest, and most powerful. The Moroccan traveler Ibn Battuta visited Mali during Sulayman's reign. He left a vivid description of the fabulous riches he observed at the *mansa's* court, including musical instruments made of precious metals:

A snake curls down the forehead of this terracotta figure of a man. In some African kingdoms, snakes symbolized divine kingship. Like the skins of a snake, divine kingship shed the lives of past kings as new kings took their place.

"Power Lies in Deeds"

GRIOT OF MALI, THE EPIC OF SUNDIATA, 13TH CENTURY

The Mandinka didn't write literary or historical works in their own languages (they used Arabic for that before about 1700). But the mansas *had griots, royal poet-historians, to memorize and recite the deeds of their ancestors. Like the ancient Greek* Iliad *and* Odyssey, *the epic of Sundiata is part history and part legend. This oral tradition has been handed down from the 13th century. In this passage, Sundiata's griot reminds him of his ancestors' accomplishments to give him heart on the eve of his battle against the Sosso.*

But listen to what your ancestors did, so that you will know what you have to do.

Bilali, the second of the name, conquered old Mali. Latal Kalabi conquered the country between the Niger and the Sankarani. By going to Mecca, Lahibatoul Kalabi, of illustrious memory, brought divine blessing upon Mali. Mamadi Kani made warriors out of hunters and bestowed armed strength upon Mali. His son Bamari Tagnokelin, the vindictive king, terrorized Mali with this army, but Maghan Kon Fatta, also called Nare Maghan, to whom you owe your being, made peace prevail and happy mothers yielded Mali a populous youth.

You are the son of Nare Maghan, but you are also the son of your mother Sogolon, the buffalo-woman, before whom powerless sorcerers shrank in fear. You have the strength and majesty of the lion, you have the might of the buffalo.

I have told you what future generations will learn about your ancestors, but what will we be able to relate to our sons so that your memory will stay alive, what will we have to teach our sons about you? What unprecedented exploits, what unheard-of feats? By what distinguished actions will our sons be brought to regret not having lived in the time of Sundiata?

Griots are men of the spoken word, and by the spoken word we give life to the gestures of kings. But words are nothing but words; power lies in deeds. Be a man of action; do not answer me any more with your mouth, but tomorrow, on the plain of Krina, show me what you would have me recount to coming generations. Tomorrow allow me to sing the "Song of the Vultures" over the bodies of the thousands of Sossos whom your sword will have laid low before evening.

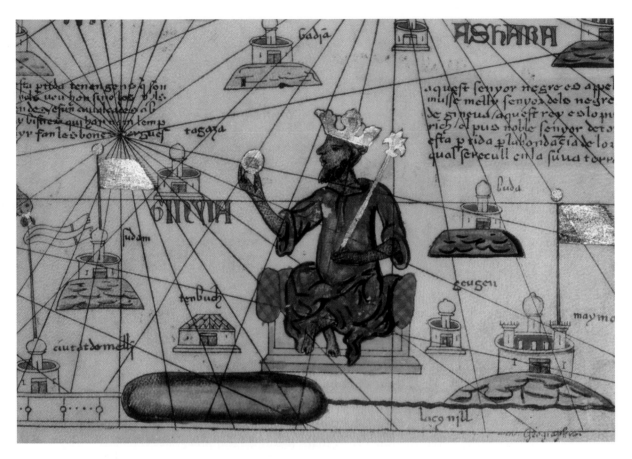

Mansa Musa's reputation as the richest king in the world reached as far as Spain, where a 14th-century cartographer portrayed him looking at an orb of pure gold.

The sultan comes out from a gate in the corner of the palace, bow in hand, his quiver between his shoulders, and on his head a cap of gold, tied with a golden band which has fringes like thin-bladed knives more than a span long. He often wears a robe which is soft and red, made from a Roman cloth. . . . The singers go out before him carrying gold and silver [guitars] and behind him come three hundred armed slaves.

Mansa Sulayman carried on Mansa Musa's policies and became almost as well known for his sponsorship of religion and scholars. Both Musa and Sulayman observed various Islamic rituals and holidays to encourage their people to follow Islam more closely. Like the caliphs of Baghdad before them, they employed court officials to enforce Islamic law and to see to it that Muslims throughout Mali observed the Five Pillars of Islam, especially prayer, fasting, and giving of alms. Ibn Battuta gave this account of Mansa Sulayman coming out to meet with his officials:

> The sultan sits on certain days in the palace yard to give audience. There is a platform with three steps under a tree. . . . It is covered with silk and has pillows placed on it. The [screen] is raised, there is a shelter made of silk with a golden bird like a sparrowhawk above it. . . . The sultan walks slowly and pauses often and sometimes he stops completely. When he comes to the [screen] he stops and looks at the people. Then he mounts the steps with dignity in the manner of a preacher getting into the pulpit. When he sits down they beat the drums, blow the bugles and the horns, and three of the slaves go out in haste and call the deputy and the [commanders of the army]. They enter and sit down. . . . [The court translator] stands at the door while the rest of the people are in the street under the tree.

Ibn Battuta met many of these people, including Islamic judges, legal scholars, Quran teachers, and preachers.

Even at the courts, powerful *mansas* such as Musa and Sulayman had to continue following some traditional Sudanese practices. According to Islamic rules, children inherit power and possessions through their father's family. But it's very likely that, before converting to Islam, the Mandinka passed things down through the mother's line. The Queen Mother occupied an official position at court and was an important figure long before the kings adopted Islam, and she continued to do so even after their conversion. The Queen Mother and the king's wives exercised power in their own right.

Ibn Battuta told an interesting story about two of Sulayman's wives that shows how Muslim and native Man-

They are very zealous in their attempt to learn the holy Quran by heart. In the event that their children are negligent in this respect, fetters are placed on the children's feet and are left until the children can recite the Quran from memory. On a holiday I went to see the judge, and seeing his children in chains, I asked him, "Aren't you going to let them go?" He answered, "I won't let them go until they know the Quran by heart."

—Ibn Battuta, describing the Muslims he met in Mali in *Travels in Asia and Africa,* 14th century

"Among the signs of his virtue are that he used to emancipate a slave every day, that he made the pilgrimage to the sacred house of God, and that in the course of his pilgrimage he built the great mosque of Timbuktu as well as the mosques of Dukurey, Gundam, Direy, Wanko, and Bako."

—An Islamic judge and scholar of Timbuktu,
description of Mansa Musa, 15th century

dinka practices worked together and sometimes clashed. According to him, the *mansa's* first wife was considered to be his full partner in ruling the land, following, as he said, "the custom of the blacks [Africans]." Following a common custom among Muslims, the sultan's first wife was also his cousin.

Once, Sulayman was angry with his first wife and cousin, Qasa, and had her confined to a house as punishment. He replaced her as first wife with his other wife, Banju. When Sulayman replaced Qasa with Banju, Qasa's sisters refused to show Banju the respect customarily given the queen. Sulayman released Qasa, but Banju complained about the lack of respect from Qasa's sisters. When the *mansa* heard this, he got angry again, and he humiliated Qasa's sisters before his entire court. Qasa rebelled and tried to form an alliance with one of her uncles in a plot to dethrone Sulayman. This was very dangerous because she had her own soldiers. Again, Sulayman discovered what was going on, and this time Qasa had to seek refuge in the house of a respected religious scholar who was able to protect her even from the king.

Despite their dedication to spreading Islam, the *mansas* never were able to conquer or convert a people called the Mossi, who eventually attacked them from the south. Unfortunately, at about the same time, a Berber people

called the Tuareg were also attacking them from the northeast. A growing rivalry among several branches of the royal
clan of Mali weakened the empire so much that it couldn't
defend itself. Mali's power faded rapidly after the end of the
14th century. Though the kingdom continued to exist in
name for several hundred more years, the Songhay Empire
came to surpass it in power and territory.

THE SONGHAY FIGHT BACK

During the 14th century, the *mansas* of Mali had captured
the Songhay city of Gao. Gao was one of the most impressive cities of the trans-Saharan trade, rivaling Awdaghost
and Kumbi Saleh in the pace of its bustling, thriving
trade. While these other towns were tied to the routes of
the western Sahara, Gao developed as the main trading
link to the central and eastern Sahara. By the 16th century, Gao was home to an exceeding number of rich
merchants, and many Africans came to buy cloth from
North Africa and Europe. The town abounded in grain
and meat for sale, as well as melons, citrus fruits, rice,
and good well water. Merchants sold slaves here, many
of them mere children. Horses were highly prized (for
use in war) and fetched high prices. Most of the rest of
the kingdom was made up of small villages where farmers lived who dressed in animal skins and sandals
made from camel skin. The kings taxed them so
much, complained one resident, that they scarcely
had anything left on which to live.

The Songhay had founded Gao and as early as
the 700s had used their great war canoes to extend
their control up the Niger River as far as the bend.
They established trading villages all along the river

*This rare 14th-century terracotta figure of a horse and rider was excavated
from an ancient grave mound. Horses were rare south of the Sahara and
had to be brought from the Maghrib, which made them expensive. Only
wealthy chiefs and kings could afford to buy a mounted cavalry, giving them
a military advantage over their subjects and enemies.*

and dominated and traded with nearby farming communities. Quite understandably, the Songhay wanted Gao back. And they took advantage of Mali's decline in the 1400s to get it.

With a powerful army of horsemen and a fleet of war canoes, Songhay's Sonni dynasty of rulers took back control of Gao and the other upstream towns. A ruler named Sonni Ali captured Timbuktu in 1468. He then extended the Songhay Empire deep into the desert to the north to include some valuable oases. To the south, he captured the prominent trading city of Jenne.

Like Sundiata, Sonni Ali is remembered as a great conqueror and the founder of his empire. Sundiata is largely remembered through the griots' oral tradition, but Sonni Ali figures in a history book written in Arabic by the 17th-century West African al-Sadi. According to al-Sadi's *History*

A 19th-century visitor from France drew this view and plan of the great mosque in Timbuktu, which had been established as a center of Islamic study 400 years before.

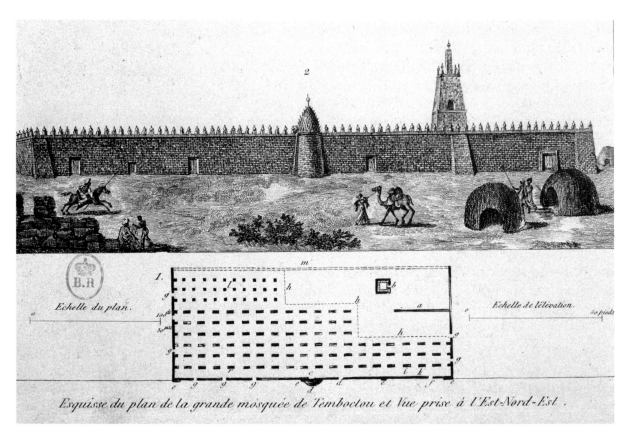

Esquisse du plan de la grande mosquée de Temboctou et Vue prise à l'Est-Nord-Est.

of the Sudan, Ali, like the early kings of Mali, seems to have mixed Islam with ancient Songhay religious beliefs. Despite being a Muslim, out of respect for the farmers, he continued to practice the old religion that emphasized magical practices and worshipping the ancestors. This greatly annoyed the *ulama* of Timbuktu, who were reluctant to submit to his authority. One 17th-century West African Muslim scholar gave this negative opinion of the Sonni ruler: "he was a man of great strength and colossal energy, a tyrant, a miscreant, an aggressor, a despot, and a butcher who killed so many human beings that only God Most High could count them." Faced with their rebellion, Ali took revenge by persecuting the scholars of Timbuktu while favoring those of Jenne, who tolerated him better. Timbuktu, however, had become a center of vast religious influence, so Sonni Ali had made some very powerful enemies.

When Ali died, one of his generals, Muhammad Turé, drove his son from the throne and seized power for himself. The *ulamas* at Timbuktu probably made that easy for him to do. Muhammad Turé founded a new line of Songhay rulers, the Askias, and became the empire's greatest head of state. He strengthened his position by tightening control over territorial chiefs and by adding to his armies professional soldiers whom he organized into units of mounted cavalry. He continued Sonni Ali's conquests to include the important salt-producing desert town of Taghaza.

Askia Muhammad Turé recognized the importance of Islam to the trade of his people. Islam provided a legal framework through which business matters could be negotiated, finalized, and enforced. And its official language, Arabic, was indispensable to long-distance trade, because it enabled people to keep written records and to correspond with business partners in distant cities. So, like the great Malian emperor Mansa Musa, Askia Muhammad Turé went on a pilgrimage to Mecca soon after he came to the throne to help reinforce his standing as a Muslim ruler.

On Askia Muhammad Turé's return, he helped revive Timbuktu as a great center of learning. According to local stories, after he returned from his pilgrimage, Mansa Musa

This list of cures from Timbuktu gives methods, including both plant and animal substances and prayers, for diagnosing and treating various illnesses. Medicine was an important field of study at Timbuktu and Jenne.

had built the Sankore mosque university at Timbuktu. From this base, Timbuktu had grown into a center of learning for all of West Africa. Beautiful handwritten manuscripts on Islamic law, theology, and local history eventually were copied in Arabic at Timbuktu and made their way into scholars' libraries all over West Africa. Many of the books still survive today.

During Askia Muhammad Turé's reign, Timbuktu reached its high point as a center of scholarship and book production. A 16th-century traveler from Spain claimed, "Here are great store of doctors, judges, priests, and other learned men, that are bountifully maintained at the king's cost and charges. And hither are brought diverse manuscripts or written books out of Barbarie [North Africa], which are sold for more money than any other merchandise."

Askia Muhammad Turé's pilgrimage and his promotion of Islamic scholarship paid off. Muslim merchants crowded into Timbuktu from all over the Sudan and the Maghrib. Not only did Songhay trade reach northward, but it reached eastward as well to include the Hausa city-states of what is now northern Nigeria. The Hausa people contributed new products to the trans-Saharan trade: kola nuts, dried or smoked fish, grain, finely tooled leather goods, and indigo-dyed cotton cloth.

Another new phenomenon in the markets of Timbuktu was an increase in the numbers of slaves traded from the forest people to the south of the African grasslands to the Muslim states of the north. Nobody knows how many slaves were traded altogether, but Ibn Battuta reported that 600 female slaves accompanied his caravan alone on his return voyage from Mali to Morocco. Over the many centuries of the Muslim trade, many, many slaves—maybe millions— were sold. As important as the slave trade became in later centuries, and with all the attention it got from European observers, very little is known about it before 1500. Muslims and other Africans wrote almost nothing about slaves and the trade since everyone took slavery for granted. Slavery was probably so common that it was "normal"; writers such as Ibn Battuta, for example, rarely were moved to comment about it. Very likely, though, people were enslaved for many reasons, including debt, war, and religion, especially with the coming of Islam. Muslims saw nothing wrong with enslaving non-Muslims. In fact, it was thought to be good because it provided an opportunity to convert people to Islam.

Songhay would enjoy a long period of good government and prosperity under Askia Muhammad. However, the Askias who followed quarreled over the succession, weakening the government. In just 70 years, Songhay had eight different rulers. Finally, the sultan of Morocco (a rival of Askia Muhammad for control of Saharan salt mines) could not resist the wealth of Songhay's trading network in the Sudan. In 1591, a Moroccan army of 4,000, armed with guns—a new weapon that the Songhay did not yet have—made the dangerous two-month crossing of the desert. The Songhay tried to negotiate with the invaders, but in the end they may have been frightened by the Moroccans'

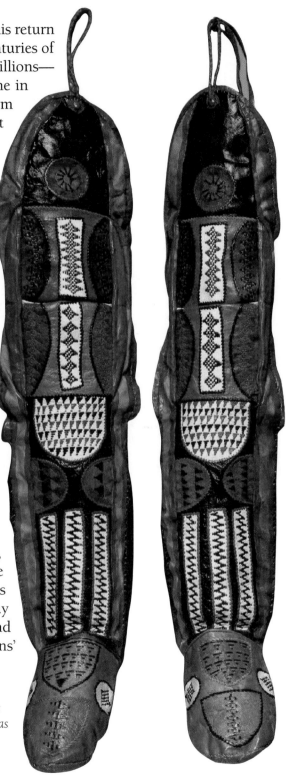

The Hausa people of northern Nigeria became known for the superb craftsmanship that went into such leather goods as these finely tooled riding boots. The Hausa traded them as far away as Morocco and Europe.

Songhay ruler Askia Muhammad is buried in this adobe pyramid-shaped tomb. Buildings in the western Sudan—even mosques and kings' tombs—were made from such readily available materials as mud, grass, and timber.

new weapon, the gun. The Moroccans defeated the Askia's army and occupied the Sudan. In the end, however, their occupation only helped to destroy much of the trade that had attracted them in the first place. Their presence increased the amount of warfare in the region, and many local producers of goods and merchants found it hard to continue doing business in a violent environment. Though other neighboring states continued to thrive, and later states would arise in this part of Africa, nobody in the Sudan would rule over such vast territories as the great Mali and Songhay empires.

CHAPTER 11

ONIS AND OBAS
THE FOREST KINGS OF WEST AFRICA

Sometime around 1000, farming and a population had blossomed to the point that a ruling class came into being at a West African forest town called Ifé. Ifé's rulers included chiefs and a king called the Oni. The Oni's power was tied to religious beliefs. His people were the Yoruba of what now is southwestern Nigeria. According to Yoruba traditions passed down orally from generation to generation, Ifé was the place where the sky god, Olorun, placed the first Yoruba man. His name was Oduduwa. The Onis of Ifé based their authority on the claim that they were the direct descendants of Oduduwa. After Islam made its way to Ifé, some Yoruba began to claim that Oduduwa, and so all Yoruba, came from Mecca.

Ifé was in a perfect spot for traders, right between the forest and the wooded grasslands on the shortest route from the tropical forest to Jenne, one of the biggest trade centers of the Sudan. The Buré and Bitu goldfields, on which the great trading cities of the Sudan depended, were in woodlands that bordered the forest. Slaves mostly came from the forest, and ivory (from elephant tusks) did too. The Sudanese also demanded kola nuts, which grew in the forest. Islam forbade alcohol and

A Bini craftsman fashioned this box, made of wood with copper and brass strips, for serving kola nuts to the Oba. The Bini people were highly skilled in the use of metals, wood, clay, and ivory.

other drug-like substances, but caffeine wasn't on the list. Kola nuts are full of caffeine.

RIVER ROUTES AND FOREST PATHS

Traders transporting goods from the forests passed through Ifé, traveling across lagoons, up river highways, and along numberless forest paths until they reached their final destination, which in most cases was a great trading center such as Jenne or Gao. Most often, the traders traveled by water, because they could ship heavy items easily by canoe. The thickly wooded terrain of the forests, especially near the coast south of the grasslands, hindered travel and communications. Fortunately, the forestlands abounded with rivers. Where there was no water route, traders often relied on professional carriers, called porters, or slaves to carry big bundles of goods. A 19th-century eyewitness reported seeing some porters carry loads of up to 180 pounds (how many of your textbooks would that be?) as far as 100 miles.

Most trade, however, was local and carried out by ordinary village people, typically women. In many forest areas, women held markets every three or four days, gathering in

As the grasslands grow toward the Equator in the middle of Africa, they give way to forests. The tropical forests around the Equator are very hot and humid and get rain every day. Buildings in the western Sudan—even mosques and kings' tombs—were made from such readily available materials as mud, grass, and timber.

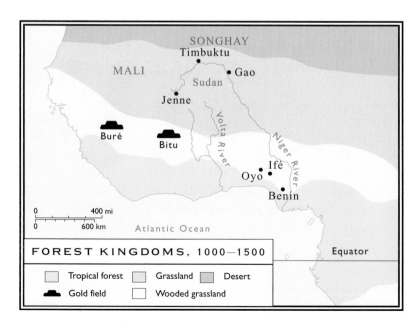

long, flowing, colorful skeins of cloth wrapped about themselves to bargain over groceries such as salted fish or meat and baskets of vegetables, yams, or grain. Gold was the most valuable item at the market, of course, along with cloth, salt, iron, and copper. Small seashells imported from East Africa, called cowries, were a common form of money, along with bars of iron or copper in standard sizes and shapes, called *manilas*.

Archaeologists have discovered some extraordinary artworks from Ifé, including this elegant terracotta head. The high productivity of Yoruba farmers enabled them to support a wealthy ruling class, which lived in towns and cities and sponsored craftsmen and artists.

Yoruba civilization was based on cities that depended on farming people who lived in the surrounding countryside for food and things to trade. This was much different from how people organized themselves in the Sudan. The Sudanic empires depended on great trading cities such as Timbuktu, but the forest kingdoms, like the city-states of ancient Greece, were organized around their capital cities. The forest cities were unusually big, sometimes covering up to 50 square miles in area.

IFÉ'S OFFSPRING AND THE OBAS OF BENIN

Even after Ifé declined around 1500, it still kept some influence among the Yoruba and their neighbors as the holy "mother city" to all Yoruba. The religious center of Ifé gave rise to new cities. One of Ifé's "children" was the city-state of Oyo, which emerged around 1400 and remained the largest and dominant Yoruba kingdom until the late 1700s. Oyo was ruled by a divine king, called the Alafin, who claimed to be descended from one of the seven sons of Oduduwa. Like

"From thence flows, as from a fountain, all the water on the face of the earth, salt as well as fresh. From thence the sun and the moon arise, where they are buried in the ground, and all the people of this country, and even white men, have come from this town."

— Church Missionary Intelligencer,
description of Ifé, 1854

other Yoruba kings, the Alafin had vast courts that included many wives, fortune-tellers, drummers and other musicians, poet-historians, bodyguards, and slaves.

The Alafin controlled a large empire, governing it through a system of local chiefs who were drawn from the local senior clans. Senior chiefs from the seven districts of the capital city formed a council that advised the Alafin and limited his power. Clan elders usually were free to govern the affairs of their clans without interference from the Alafin. All the most important religious and political leaders belonged to a secret religious society, called the Ogboni, which had the right to review decisions made by the Alafin and his council, such as decisions to make alliances, go to war, or conclude peace treaties with enemies.

According to oral tradition, Oyo's Alafin were the cousins of the rulers of a place called Benin. Benin's first divine king, called the Oba, had been sent west from Ifé in the 13th century when a council of chiefs asked Oduduwa to send them one of his sons to be their ruler.

This 18th-century brass casting of a horn blower comes out of a centuries-old tradition of metal casting at Benin. Musicians often accompanied the Oba, or king, on trips outside the palace, and such figures were often displayed on altars to departed ancestors in the Benin royal court.

Many of Benin's kingship traditions are similar to those of Ifé—both use court jesters and ceremonial swords made from gold and brass as symbols of kingly authority. But the people of Benin, called Bini, were not Yoruba. Because the Bini language is so old and differs so much from the Yoruba language, scholars of African languages believe that the Bini have lived in their present homeland for thousands of years.

According to Bini traditions, their first king arrived about 1300 or a little earlier. As a matter of fact, archaeologists who have worked at Benin City have uncovered a complicated system of earthen walls and ditches that surrounded the early city and dates approximately to—you guessed it—1300.

Sometime in the 1400s, an Oba named Ewuare (which means, "It is cool" or "The trouble has ended") came to power. Like the great kings of Mali and Songhay, Ewuare engaged in frequent wars of expansion. He seized control of Yoruba land to the west and other territories to the east to greatly add to the size of the Benin Empire. Ewuare expanded the boundaries of Benin City and built new walls to enclose nearby villages within the city's precincts. According to Bini oral tradition, "He fought against and captured 201 towns and villages at Ekiti, Ikare, Kukuruku, Eka and the Ibo country on this side of the Niger River. He took their petty rulers captive and caused the people to pay tribute to him." By 1500, the city had become enormous, about seven miles across at its broadest point, with the palace of

continued on page 136

"Ewuare was a great magician, physician, traveler and warrior."

—Bini oral tradition, probably 15th–16th century,
recorded by Chief Jacob Egharevba,
A Short History of Benin, 1934

Please Take Good Care of These Seven Lice

**BENIN ORAL TRADITION, 12TH CENTURY, RECORDED BY
CHIEF JACOB EGHAREVBA, A SHORT HISTORY OF BENIN, 1934**

People in West Africa often learned their history from storytellers, who specialized in memorizing and reciting everything about the past. They could recite the names of kings and their children, the victories and defeats in battles, and even the exact words of the soldiers who fought in the wars. These reciters of history—sometimes called griots—knew so much that they became trusted advisers of rulers. Eventually, in our own time, the stories were written down. This particular history, written down in 1934, describes the ways in which the Bini in the 12th century sent to the city of Ifé for a ruler. It also draws lessons from that history about how responsible leaders need to judge situations and behave.

[T]he people . . . sent an ambassador to the Oni Odudua, the great and wisest ruler of Ifé, asking him to send one of his sons to be their ruler. For things were getting from bad to worse and the people saw that there was need for a capable ruler.

In order to test the ability of the Bini to look after his son, Odudua first of all sent seven lice to the Benin chiefs to be cared for and returned after three years. This condition was fulfilled and Odudua was greatly surprised to see the lice in increased sizes when they were sent back to him by the chiefs. He exclaimed that "the people who can take care of such minute pests as lice can undoubtedly take care of my son." . . .

Before he could send his son to Benin, Odudua died, but he left strong orders to his son and successor . . . that Oranmiyan should be sent there. So Prince Oranmiyan, one of the sons of Odudua of Ifé, the father and progenitor of the Yoruba Obas, was sent, accompanied by courtiers, including Ogiefa, a native doctor, and he succeeded in reaching the city after much trouble at Ovia River with the ferryman.

[The Benin governor] was much opposed to his coming. . . . But as the need for a proper Oba was felt to be so great by the inhabitants, no heed was paid to his advice.

Prince Oranmiyan took up his abode in the palace built for him . . . by the elders. Soon after his arrival he married a beautiful lady . . . by whom he had a son. After some years residence here he called a meeting of the people and renounced his office remarking that the country was a land of vexation, . . . and that only a child born, trained, and educated in the arts and mysteries of the land could reign over the people. He caused his son . . . to be made Oba in his place, and returned to his native land, Ifé, leaving Ogiefa . . . and others at Benin in charge of his son.

Two court officials support an Oba, who has mudfish for feet in this brass casting. The mudfish (or crayfish) represented the divinity of the Oba, since he was supposedly able to walk on water.

continued from page 133

the Oba at its very heart. The population probably numbered in the hundreds of thousands, making Benin by far the largest city in sub-Saharan Africa. According to oral tradition, Ewuare "made good roads in Benin city. . . . In fact the town rose to importance and gained the name 'city' during his reign."

Reciters of Bini oral tradition say that Ewuare "was . . . powerful, courageous and [wise]." One of his wise moves was to appoint ordinary citizens of the capital to a royal council, along with the old clan chiefs. He ranked the chiefs and assigned specific governing powers to each one. In doing so, he took some of the inherited power within the kingdom away from the old clan elders and made them dependent on his authority. Euware's successors benefited from this move, which made the monarchy more powerful. By the 16th century, a British visitor to Benin reported,

> [W]hen his noblemen are in [the Oba's] presence, they never look him in the face, but sit cowering, . . . so they move upon their buttocks with their elbows upon their knees and their hands before their faces, not looking up until the king commands them. And when they are coming toward the king, as far as they do see him they do show such reverence, sitting on the ground with their faces covered as before. Likewise, when they depart from him, they turn not their backs toward him, but go creeping backward with like reverence.

The Obas ordered brass and bronze castings to be made as permanent "records" of their reigns. They depicted the Obas in different ways, showing them as godlike beings ruling over nature or as kings seated and surrounded by their officials. Castings also depicted other court officials, including the Queen Mother, the official royal historian and praise-singer, the royal drummer, the guardians of the gates to the palace, generals, chiefs, and powerful clan

Their princes and noblemen used to [prick] and raise their skins with pretty knots in diverse forms, as it were branched damask. . . . And albeit they go in manner all naked, yet are many of them, and especially their women, in manner laden with collars, bracelets, hoops and chains, either of gold, copper, or ivory. I myself have one of their bracelets of ivory, weighing two pound and six ounces. . . . This one of their women did wear upon her arm. It is made of one whole piece of the biggest part of the [tusk] turned and somewhat carved, with a hole in the midst, wherein they put their hands to wear it on their arm.

—British merchant Richard Eden, describing Bini tattoos and jewelry, *Decades of the New World*, 1555

"[T]he king . . . sat in a great huge hall, long and wide, the walls made of earth without windows, the roof of thin boards, open in sundry places . . . to let in the air."

—British merchant Richard Eden, description of the Oba's court, *Decades of the New World*, 1555

elders. Animals, too, were a favorite subject of the artists, whose creations were displayed on the walls of the king's palace.

Benin oral traditions say the art of bronze and brass casting, like the kingship, came to Benin from Ifé. One king in particular, Oguola, is given credit for bringing these skills to Benin. A Benin chief tells us that "Oba Oguola wished to introduce brass-casting into Benin so as to produce works of art similar to those sent him from Ifé. He therefore sent to the Oni of Ifé for a brass-smith and Iguegha was sent to him."

The Benin bronzes tell us a lot about the nature of Benin kingship. Like the kings of Ifé and Oyo, the Oba of Benin was a divine king, meaning that he was credited with god-like powers that the Bini people thought were critical to the welfare of the kingdom. In one bronze, the Oba is portrayed as having the feet of a mudfish, or crayfish, which symbolized the belief that the Oba had power over water that allowed him to walk on it. The python was also a symbol of the Obas. It reflected the Bini belief that the divine kingship was eternal but that individual kings had to die, just as the snake sheds its skin.

Two Portuguese soldiers riding on horseback decorate this carved ivory salt cellar. The Bini made such objects as souvenirs for the Europeans who visited them. Salt was rare and highly prized among the forest people of West Africa.

CHAPTER 12

THERE'S TREASURE IN THOSE HILLS!

GREAT ZIMBABWE AND THE SHONA OF SOUTHERN AFRICA

In southeastern Africa, on a high plateau between two rivers, there lived a farmer who spent his days on the savannah growing millet and sorghum. He lived in a small village with his family and fellow farmers. Ironworkers in the village supplied the farmers with tools to make their intense labor just a little easier. The people in this village were connected to villages scattered throughout the plateau by their way of life and by a common language called Bantu.

The Bantu-speakers (or Bantu for short) placed great value on their families, clans, and friendships. The farmer's parents had taught him that his fellow clan members and friends mattered perhaps even more than he did as an individual. Bantu families depended on themselves to make most things they needed, and they produced their own food. But they also knew they could rely on other clan members, or kin, to help them out in times of need. It simply was expected, and there was no shame in it.

In the many villages across the plateau, life centered on people's daily lives of growing food and of honoring their elders and ancestors. However, the Bantu's story also concerns states and kingdoms, just like the rest of Africa.

At some point, the farmer's descendants began to acquire and hoard cows. Although crop growing was still the people's main source of food, cattle were valuable because they provided milk and meat that people could depend on in drought years, when the usual crop foods were in short supply. The Bantu started using cows like money, exchanging them for other items or offering them as gifts. As the Bantu became richer from cattle herding, they began building more and more with stone, and some lucky people moved into grand houses that were much larger than the Bantu had ever built before. And, of course, they constructed stone enclosures for their precious cattle. On three flat-topped hills in eastern Botswana, archaeologists have discovered the remains of large settlements that existed between 650 and 1300. Here the Bantu built big, circular, thatched houses around central enclosures, or kraals, which were used to contain herds of cattle.

Improvements in houses and cattle enclosures didn't necessarily mean that the living was easy for cattle herders. Raising cattle requires land. Cattle breeders started to squabble over the land, and soon they needed to call in someone, a third party, to settle their differences. That third party needed to have some power to enforce his decisions. This might be how the Bantu first started to have chiefs. Early settlements appeared to have been the centers of chiefships, because many smaller villages surrounded them. Suddenly there was a rift between people who ate sorghum and game and people who ate beef. The people who lived in the big villages could afford the luxury of eating beef rather than game animals. A little after 1000, they also started to enjoy the luxury of goods imported from across the seas, such as Chinese porcelains, Indian beads, and beautiful Persian and Arab pots.

Such items passed through the hands of many traders who lived in the lands between Africa's eastern Swahili coast and the Shona people of the interior, who descended from the Bantu. Just about the time when gold began playing a bigger part in the coastal trade, regions to the west of the plateau steadily began producing the precious metal. In his manuscript, *The Meadows of Gold*, the 10th-century Arab geographer al-Masudi mentions an inland people who produced gold "and many other wonderful things," such as iron

Using only hand tools, expert Shona stonemasons cut and squared the stones for these walls from solid rock. The builders used no mud or cement in the walls' construction and built them up in places to a height of four stories.

Who Seweth the Heavens Like Cloth

" **HYMN TO MWARI, RAIN GOD OF THE SHONA, SOMETIME AFTER 600**

This hymn probably was sung by the spirit mediums or priests of Mwari, the most important god of the Shona people, as a way of appealing to Mwari. Mwari seems to have been both the high god as well as the god of rain. Rain was important to the Shona since it ensured that their crops would be plentiful.

Great Spirit!
Piler up of rocks into towering mountains!
When thou stampest on the stone,
The dust rises and fills the land.
Hardness of the precipice;
Waters of the pool that turn
Into misty rain when stirred.
Vessel overflowing with oil!...
Who seweth the heavens like cloth:
Let him knit together that which is below.
Caller forth of the branching trees:
Thou bringest forth the shoots
That they stand erect.
Thou has filled the land with mankind,
The dust rises on high, oh Lord!
Wonderful One, thou livest
In the midst of the sheltering rocks,
Thou givest of rain to mankind:
We pray to thee,
Hear us, Lord!
Show mercy when we beseech thee, Lord.
Thou art on high with the spirits of the great.
Thou raisest the grass-covered hills
Above the earth, and createst,
Gracious One.

Mwari was associated with a bird called a fish eagle, which migrated to Shonaland at the beginning of the rainy season every year.

and ivory. Al-Masudi also reported that he witnessed the people riding cattle like horses.

Between about 1100 and 1300, an inland settlement called Mapungubwe became an important supplier of gold to the gold-exporting cities of Sofala and Kilwa on the coast. In Mapungubwe, a wealthy ruling class lived in sturdy, mud-and-wood houses on top of a hill, with a cattle kraal dominating it. They built stone terraces on hillsides to conserve precious runoff from rainwater. Elephant hunters pursued the animals for their ivory. Miners excavated copper from sources nearby, and metalsmiths hammered gold, brought from mines to the west, into foil-thin sheets used to cover wood figures found in the rulers' houses. Archaeological finds from the site of Mapungubwe—beads made from shells and glass, brightly dyed cotton cloth, and Chinese porcelain—all point to trade as a major source of the wealth and power for the rulers of the settlement.

CITY MADE OF STONE: GREAT ZIMBABWE

But of all the inland kingdoms, Great Zimbabwe represented the height of development. Given similarities in the stone-cutting technologies and construction techniques, it appears to have been built by the same people who built Mapungubwe, people who are the ancestors of today's Shona people. These early Shona founded Great Zimbabwe around 1100, and between 1200 and 1400, it became the center of a large and prosperous Shona kingdom.

The word *zimbabwe* means "stone buildings" in the Shona language, and it referred especially to structures where its kings lived and were buried. The people at Mapungubwe had used stones to construct hillside terraces, and the people at Great Zimbabwe and other *zimbabwes* used that technology to build highly elaborate walls. In the 1500s, Portuguese explorers saw what these buildings looked like before they fell into ruin. One of them noted that the structures had by then become part of Shona legend:

> The natives of the country call these edifices
> Symbaoe [*zimbabwes*], which according to their

language signifies [a] court, for every place where [a royal court] might be is so called. . . . When and by whom these edifices were [built] . . . there is no record, but they say they are the work of the [spirits], for in comparison with their power and knowledge it does not seem possible to them that they should be the work of man.

Two major buildings still stand at Great Zimbabwe: a hilltop structure that later archaeologists called the Acropolis, after the Greek word for "high city," and a second, somewhat later structure in the valley below called the Great Enclosure. The kings probably lived first in the hilltop Acropolis and then around 1400 built the gigantic walls of the Great Enclosure and moved their mud-and-wood houses inside it. They built many other stone walls constructed outside the Great Enclosure, and eventually the entire valley in which it stood was filled with the hundreds, maybe thousands, of houses of the common people. These houses were built of solid mud over wooden frames. Poles on the outside of a house supported its cone-shaped roof. These buildings at Great Zimbabwe stood at the center of an extensive empire that might have covered most of the inland plateau. Many other stone *zimbabwes* were built all over the plateau on which lesser chiefs and members of the ruling clan might have lived.

SHONA CIVILIZATION, 1000–1500

Most of the long-distance trade between the gold and copper mines to the west passed through the capital city at Great Zimbabwe. There, the government collected taxes on the metals before they were sent to Sofala, where the Swahili merchants of Kilwa and other communities traded for them. The centuries in which Great Zimbabwe was at its peak development coincided precisely with the time when Kilwa dominated the coastal trade (and during which Ibn Battuta visited it). The kings at Great Zimbabwe became wealthy from this trade, and they lived in luxury, adorning themselves with gold and copper ornaments, consuming great quantities of beef from the royal herds, and eating off fine plates imported from Persia and China. Because cotton cloth was so rare, the ruling class greatly prized the textile that came from India, and they used it as a symbol of their prestige and power.

Sometime between 1400 and 1450, Great Zimbabwe was abandoned for unknown reasons. One possibility is

All that remains of the city of Great Zimbabwe is its stone walls. More than six centuries ago, hundreds of mud-and-timber huts stood, and possibly thousands of farmers, traders, miners, and royal family members lived, worked, and enjoyed life among these now-silent walls.

The king of Great Zimbabwe and his family built their houses within these walls, called the Great Enclosure. The stone tower (right) resembles a place where grain was stored; it was probably important in fertility rituals.

that the region around it became overpopulated and the dry, fragile environment could no longer support so many people. According to Shona oral tradition, a shortage of salt caused the last king of Great Zimbabwe, Mutota, to abandon the great city and to conquer another region to the north called Dande. By the 1400s, too, African miners had discovered new sources of gold on the northern part of the Shona plateau. So both farmers and miners would have had reason to abandon their homes in the central and southern parts and relocate to the north.

OF KINGS AND GOLD MINERS

Aside from oral tradition and archaeological evidence, history is silent about what life was like for these kings and their subjects. Scholars can only make educated guesses based on the writings of 16th- and 17th-century eyewitnesses who visited the later Shona kingdoms. Most written records come from the period after the Portuguese arrived in East Africa in the 1500s. But even these records tell very little about what life was like for most people in Shona kingdoms. The Portuguese talk mostly about the two things that interested them most: the kings and their courts, and where and how the Africans obtained the gold. In a letter written to the king of Portugal in 1506, a Portuguese traveler described the Shona mining operations:

> [T]hey dig out the earth and make a kind of tunnel, through which they go under the ground [to the

depth of] a long stone's throw, and keep on taking out from the veins with the ground mixed with the gold, and when collected, they put it in a pot, and cook it much in fire; and after cooking they take it out, and put it to cool, and when cold the earth remains, and the gold is all fine gold . . . and no man can take [any of it] with out leave from the king, under penalty of death.

By the 15th century, Swahili traders from the coast had begun to use the Zambezi River as a way of traveling to Shonaland and trading directly with its people rather than relying on the old routes through Great Zimbabwe. Later, Portuguese reports mentioned "fairs" (markets) that were held under the king's authority at various locations throughout the northern kingdom. There, the Europeans traded for gold, and "this gold was purchased for cloth, glass beads, and other things of no value among us," according to one Portuguese author. Apparently, Great Zimbabwe was abandoned not only for environmental reasons but also because the trade on which the kings based their power had also relocated north.

A Portuguese traveler who visited East Africa in the 16th century described meeting these later chiefs of Mwenemutapa, the new Shona capital. He reported that

[T]hey were black men [who] go naked save that they cover [themselves] with cotton cloth from the waist down. Some are clad in the skins of wild beasts, and some, the most noble, wear capes of these skins with tails . . . as a token of state and dignity. They leap as they go, and sway their bodies so as to make these tails fly from one side to the other. They carry swords thrust into wooden [sheaths] bound with much gold and other metals. . . . These are warlike men, and some too are great traders.

Eventually, the king of Great Zimbabwe, Mutota, conquered the northern capital, and his successor, Matope, extended it and opened trade with the coast. They soon extended their power over the northern Shona people. They took the title of Mwenemutapa ("master pillager") and established a powerful new state called Karanga. Foreigners who visited the kingdom, such as the Portuguese and the Swahili, confused the name of the land with the king and called the kingdom Mwenemutapa. In some ways the kingdom was probably modeled on the earlier one of Great Zimbabwe.

The Portuguese historian Manuel de Faria y Sousa, regarded as one of the most learned men of early-17th-century Portugal, wrote an account of the kingdom of Karanga that was based on information collected during an expedition in 1569. Despite the late date, scholars believe that much of this account describes customs that had been features of court life among the Shona kingdoms for several centuries beforehand, perhaps even at Great Zimbabwe itself. He notes, in particular, the specific titles and duties that were assigned to each of the "principal officers about the king." Like the earlier kings, the Mwenemutapa had many wives and officials, including a

governor of the [subject] kingdoms; . . . captain-general [of the army]; . . . great steward, to [whom] it belongs when . . . the king's principal wife, dies, to name another in her stead, but it must be

At bedtime, the Shona rested their heads on raised "pillows," such as this one carved from hardwood. Hardwood headrests are found all over Africa.

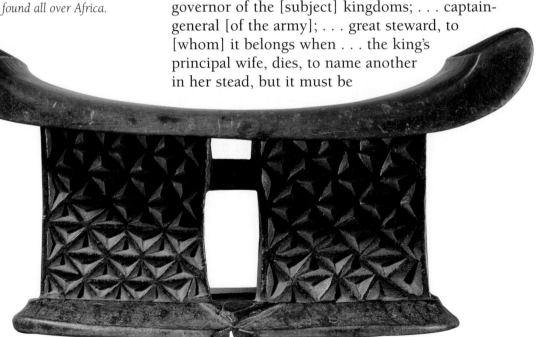

one of the king's sisters or nearest relations; . . . the head musician, who has many under him, and is a great lord; . . . captain of the [guards]; . . . the king's right hand; . . . the chief conjuror [magician]; . . . the apothecary that keeps the ointments and utensils for sorcery; [and] . . . chief porter.

Faria y Sousa recorded,

[T]he king has many wives, only nine called great queens, which are his sisters or near relations, others the daughters of nobles. The chiefest is called Mazarira. . . . Each of them lives apart, [in] as great a state as the king, and have several revenues and king-doms for their expense. As soon as one dies, another succeeds in place and name. They have power to reward and punish, as well as the king.

The kingdom of Mwenemutapa continued to dominate the inland trade and remained powerful well into the 17th century. However, the Portuguese seized control of the coastal trade in the 16th century, and almost immediately Mwenemutapa began to decline. Matters grew worse for the Shona and their Swahili trading partners in the 1600s when the Portuguese, like the Swahili before them, reached Mwenemutapa by way of the Zambezi Valley and took all the wealth for themselves. The Portuguese imposed impossible taxes on the trade. Furthermore, Portuguese Roman Catholic missionaries mistreated Shona and Swahili alike out of disdain for their native religions. In taking the king's source of income, the Portuguese had also taken away his power. Gradually, by the late 1600s, their kingdom fell apart as, one by one, the provincial chiefs renounced their positions. Today, only the ruins of the stone settlements of their kings remain as evidence of their former glory.

And, Sir, a man might go from Sofala to a city which is called Zumubany [Zimbabwe] which is large, in which the king always resides, in ten or twelve days, if you travel as in Portugal; but because they do not travel except from morning until midday, and eat and sleep until the next morning, when they go on again, they cannot go to this city in less than twenty or twenty-four days; and in the whole kingdom . . . gold is extracted.

—Diogo de Alçacova to the king of Portugal, letter, November 20, 1506

CHAPTER 13

THE EMPEROR'S GIRAFFE
EAST AFRICA'S SWAHILI COAST

Once upon a time, goes an old Swahili story, a band of Persian Muslims called the Shirazi left their hometown and sailed across the Indian Ocean in seven ships. They landed on the coast of East Africa, where the passengers of each ship founded a different city. The names of the East African cities differ in the many versions of the story that exist, but the list typically includes Shanga, Manda, Zanzibar, Mafia, and Kilwa. In a story recorded by an unknown 16th-century author, the Persians bought the island of Kilwa for a rather strange price:

> When [the Shirazi] arrived in the ship that went to Kilwa, they found it was an island surrounded by the sea. . . . They disembarked and met a man who was a Muslim. . . .
>
> They asked the Muslim about the country and he replied: "The island is ruled by an infidel from Muli [the African mainland] who is king of it; he has gone to Muli to hunt, but will return soon." After a few days the infidel returned from Muli and crossed to the island at low tide. . . . The newcomer [the Persian leader] said: "I would like to settle on the island: pray sell it to me that I may do so." The infidel answered: "I will sell it on condition that you encircle the island with colored clothing." The newcomer agreed with the infidel and bought it on the condition stipulated. He encircled the island with clothing, some

Archaeologists found this ship's prow in the shape of a bird's head in the harbor of Mombasa, a city on the coast of East Africa. It is from an Arab trading vessel called a dhow.

white, some black, and every other color besides. So the infidel agreed and took away all the clothing, handing over the island and departing for Muli.

Once in East Africa, the Persians married local African women, according to this story, and produced a mixed Afro-Arab people, the Swahili.

Except for the clothes scattered all over the beaches of Kilwa, this story seems like a reasonable explanation of how the islands came to be settled. It even says that the Persians left their homeland because of a religious dispute, just like the Pilgrims who left England for North America. The problem is that there are other stories that make different claims. Some say that Arabs were the first to settle the coastal towns after coming from Mecca, Damascus, or the great port city of Daybul in India. In one version, recorded by a 16th-century Portuguese historian, the first settlers were a band of Shiites who arrived from southwest Arabia, and "From their entrance, like a slow plague . . . worked their way along the coast, occupying new towns." Still other stories say the original settlers came from China or Portugal. So which one is true?

Actually, none. Experts in the study of languages have figured out that the Swahili-speaking peoples of the East African coast are the descendants of a group of Africans called the Bantu (or, more accurately, Bantu-speakers). The Swahili are, in fact, Africans. The Bantu migrated from West Africa beginning about 4,000 years ago and eventually came to populate most of Africa south of the Equator. Around 200, some migrated to the East African coast, and most people in East Africa, including the Swahili, are their descendants. We know this because the Swahili language is a Bantu language.

If the Swahili were African in origin, why did they hand down stories saying that they came from other places? Archaeologists have discovered the remains of mosques, locally made copper and silver coins with Arabic inscriptions, and graves that are clearly those of Muslims because the bodies were buried facing the direction of Mecca. All of this evidence proves that Muslims were living on the East African coast around the time when the caliph al-Mansur was building Baghdad in the late 700s. By about 1200, most Swahili town dwellers had converted to Islam, judging by the increasing numbers of towns with mosques, mosques in each town, and Islamic burials. The Islamic Swahili began to say they were Arab because they considered it impressive to come from the birthplace of Muhammad.

SWAHILI DAYS

As a Muslim child in Kilwa in 1498, you'd go to school to learn the Quran from a teacher called a *mwalimu*. After that, if you were a girl, you'd spend most of your time in the house helping your mother, your father's other wives (as a Muslim, he could have up to four), and a household slave or two with the housework and the cooking. Your house and the houses of your aunts, uncles, and cousins would be

The Great Mosque at Kilwa is built out of blocks of coral and a coral-based plaster. Coral grows on the ocean floor near the East African seashore.

built together in the same neighborhood. They might even have been joined together to look like modern condominiums.

All the houses had flat roofs, and some were up to three stories high. The walls of your house, like the other houses in Kilwa, were built from carved blocks of coral covered with a coral lime plaster that gave them a smooth white finish that shone in the sun. For decoration, Swahili craftsmen carved cable, chain-link, fish bone, or other patterns into some of the blocks. They also mixed coral lime with egg whites and used the wet mixture to carve intricate designs around the doors and in niches in the walls of your house.

Pleasing to the Sight

❝ **JOÃO DE BARROS, DA ASIA, AROUND 1580**

Portuguese writer João de Barros never actually saw the beautiful towns of the Swahili coast. As the king of Portugal's first professional librarian and archivist, he began collecting written reports and stories from the men and women who visited East Africa and other Portuguese settlements in the country's vast Indian Ocean empire. He used these to write Da Asia, *the most complete history of Portuguese journeys in the Indian Ocean of the 16th century. By taking such writings together with the archaeological ruins of medieval Swahili towns, historians can picture how they must have looked.*

Portuguese explorer Vasco da Gama made a habit of stopping over in East African ports such as Malindi and Mozambique on his voyages between Portugal and India. Friendly East Africans, like the sultans of Malindi, supplied him with water, vegetables, fruits, and meat.

The greater number of the houses are built of stone and mortar, with flat roofs, and at the back there are orchards planted with fruit trees and palms to give shade and please the sight as well as for their fruit. The streets are [as] narrow as those orchards are large, this being the custom among the Moors [Swahili], that they may be better able to defend themselves. Here the streets are so narrow that one can jump from one roof to the other on the opposite side. At one point of the town the king had his palace, built in the style of a fortress, with towers and turrets and every kind of defense, with a door opening to the quay to allow of entrance from the sea, and another large door on the side of the fortress that opened on the town. Facing it was a large open space where they hauled the vessels up.

"We came to Mambasa [Mombasa], a large island two days' journey by sea from the Swahili country. It possesses no territory on the mainland. They have fruit trees on the island, but no cereals, which have to be brought to them from the Swahili. Their food consists chiefly of bananas and fish."

—Ibn Battuta, *Travels in Asia and Africa*, 14th century

You wouldn't have much furniture dusting to do, because furnishings were few and simple: perhaps a few tables and carved chairs, carved beds, and woven mats. You'd spend a lot of time in the private women's rooms toward the back of house and in the courtyard. That's where the stove was. The courtyard would be fragrant with the smells of coconut, coconut milk, banana, mango, milk, rice, fish, chicken, mutton, goat, and lots of spices.

If you were a boy, once you finished Quran school, you'd start learning to be a farmer, fisherman, trader, or maybe some combination of the three. Once you grew to be a man, you'd probably spend part of your time on your nearby *shamba*, or farm, where you'd grow crops such as coconuts, mangoes, and bananas for the courtyard at home. You might also have other farms for growing millet, sorghum, or rice. Not many individuals owned the actual land back then, only the rights to it, and those would have been passed on from your family to you or your wife.

Chances are you also run a trade business. From about November to April every year, trade winds, called the northeasterly monsoon, blow ships from Arabia, the Persian Gulf, and western India across the Indian Ocean to the cities of the coast. From their merchants, you purchase Indian-made cloth and glass beads, Persian pots or Chinese porcelains, carpets, and other manufactured goods. In return, you give the gold, ivory, hides, timber, grain, iron, or slaves you have traded from your inland African customers.

You also have some time every day to spend in the nearby neighborhood mosque, praying and exchanging news and gossip with other men of the quarter. Life is so much more comfortable for you and your family than it was for your ancestors. When they first began living along the coast, around 350–650, the Bantu-speakers had to adjust to their new marine environment. From new words added to the Bantu language around this time, linguists can tell that they learned to eat coconut, fish, shellfish, and turtles;

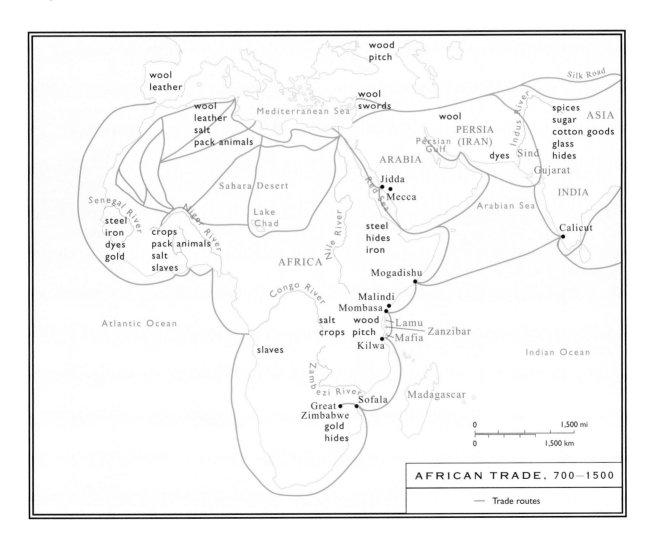

AFRICAN TRADE, 700–1500

— Trade routes

make nets and seagoing canoes; and trade with merchants from Arabia, Persia, and India. By about 1000–1200, the Swahili had learned how to mine the offshore reefs for coral as a building material; build rectangular houses from mud, coral, and coconut fronds; and build oceangoing ships.

From about 700 to 1200, the Arab and Persian ships that sailed from the Persian Gulf brought to the Swahili dates, pottery, cloth, and other manufactured items. The most popular items the traders bought from the Swahili were such animal products as hides, ivory, and rhinoceros horn, as well as amber, iron, and a type of semiprecious stone called quartz crystal. The Swahili concentrated on making iron, and one early Arab author noted that they exported a lot of it:

> The inhabitants [of the coast] are poor and wretched, and have no other means of livelihood than iron-working. There are, in fact, a great number of iron mines in the mountains of Sofala. The people of the Zanedj [coastal] Islands and other neighboring

Just inland from the East African coast, there is plenty of good land, and rainfall levels are high enough to support the cultivation of millet, rice, and vegetables, as in these fields. Coconut trees, mangoes, and bananas grow along the shore, and the coral reefs are home to abundant varieties of fish, turtles, and shellfish.

islands . . . come here for iron, which they carry to the continent and islands of India, where they sell it at a good price, for it is a material of great trade and consumption in India.

The early Swahili also made beads from seashells, which they traded to their African neighbors, and they imported Indian cotton cloth, Persian pottery, and even a little Chinese porcelain. Most of the time, they thought these articles were so precious that they used them for display as a sign of wealth and prestige. Some people even had their tombs decorated with them.

GOLDEN AGE OF CITY-STATES

You are lucky to live in the golden age of Swahili civilization, a period that began in 1200 and will end around 1500. New discoveries of gold in the region around Great Zimbabwe, deep in the interior of East Central Africa, have greatly expanded trade, both with the African interior and with the lands across the Indian Ocean. By the time the Portuguese explorer Vasco da Gama arrives in East Africa in 1498, the Swahili are part of a Muslim trade network that reaches all the way to China. Sometimes, whole animals are exported. A Chinese painting from the 15th century shows a giraffe that the Swahili gave as a gift to the Chinese emperor.

By the 1300s and 1400s, Kilwa had become one of many Swahili city-states. Unlike the empires in the Sudan, Swahili civilization never became a centralized kingdom, with just one king and one capital city. Rather, it always was a civilization of city-states. A city-state was usually made up of a major port and trading city, such as Malindi, Mombasa, or Kilwa, and several smaller nearby towns that supplied the "capital" city with food and articles of trade. These mini-states competed with each other for trade, alliances with neighbors, or control of farmlands on the African mainland or interior—and sometimes even warred among themselves. Because of their reliance on trade, the coastal towns had to have close ties with their neighbors. The Swahili

Any merchant who comes to Mombasa and brings 1,000 pieces of cloth pays to the king duties of entrance for each 1,000 pieces of cloth one mitical of gold; and then they divide the 1,000 pieces of cloth into two halves; and the king takes one half; and the other half remains to the merchant; and, whether he carries them beyond, or sells them in the city, he has to take this half to the king; and the king sends his to be sold at Sofala or Kilwa.

—Diogo de Alcacova to the king of Portugal, letter, November 20, 1506

This large Chinese jar was found in Mombasa. It dates from the Song period in China, from 906 to 1275. Swahili-speaking people imported Chinese pottery when their trade network extended from the western Indian Ocean to East Asia. It's extremely unlikely that Chinese and East African merchants traded directly with each other. Indian, Persian, or Arab merchants probably acted as middlemen.

depended on other African communities to provide them with most of the items they exported to India, Arabia, and Persia, especially animal products and gold. And the Swahili towns needed to maintain good relations with neighboring non-Muslim people so that they could farm mainland areas safely.

Throughout the 14th and 15th centuries, Kilwa was the most prosperous and powerful city-state of all. It was much nearer than any of its rivals to the biggest source of gold and ivory, Great Zimbabwe, which was located hundreds of miles inland to the south. Kilwa's greatness rested on its control of the gold trade.

In the early 14th century, a Yemeni clan migrated to Kilwa and established a sultanate there. Under Sultan Hasan bin Sulayman, the dynasty extended its control to the southern port city of Sufala, along with Zanzibar and Mafia. From the port of Sufala, the valuable gold and ivory of Zimbabwe were exported. From 1331 to 1332, world traveler Ibn Battuta was in East Africa, where he visited Hasan bin Sulayman in Kilwa. Ibn Battuta wrote:

> The majority of its inhabitants are . . . jet-black in color, and with tattoo marks on their faces. I was told by a merchant that the town of Sufala lies a fortnight's journey [south] from Kulwa [Kilwa] and that gold dust is brought to Sufala from Yufi in the country of the Limis, which is a month's journey dis-

tant from it. Kulwa is a very fine and substantially built town. . . . Its inhabitants are constantly engaged in military expeditions, for their country is contiguous to the heathen Zanj.

Ibn Battuta recorded

[The sultan] was noted for his gifts and generosity. He used to devote the fifth part of the booty made on his expeditions to pious and charitable purposes, as is prescribed in the Quran, and I have seen him give the clothes off his back to a mendicant [beggar] who asked him for them.

Kilwa apparently was a grand sight to behold in its heyday. Ibn Battuta said Kilwa was one of the most beautiful cities he had ever seen. The sultan's Husuni Kubwa palace might have been the loveliest building in sub-Saharan Africa. Seen from the sea, its smooth, white, coral lime–plastered walls and turrets stood out against a green background of palm trees. The building was up to three stories high. The sultan and his family lived in the front half, and a

The ruins of Kilwa's Husuni Kubwa directly face the Indian Ocean. The Abu'l-Mawahib sultans built the great palace and warehouse in the 15th century to house their families and to conduct trade. Quite possibly Ibn Battuta visited ibn Sulayman in this palace.

There could be seen a magnificent
City with many noble edifices
Marking the whole curve of the bay,
A landmark visible for many miles,
And ruled by a king of great antiquity;
Mombasa it is named, both isle and city.

—Portuguese poet Luiz Vaz de Camões, *The Lusiads,* an epic poem, 1572

large warehouse area for trade goods lay behind their personal rooms. Several staircases led from the beach before it, where ships unloaded their cargoes, up to the palace itself. There were several courtyards and audience chambers where the sultan received visitors, as well as an eight-sided bathing pool.

Mosques and tombs at Kilwa were made from materials similar to houses. A typical town had several mosques, and most had at least a community mosque where everyone was expected to pray together on Friday, the Muslim Sabbath. As the town grew and as the Muslim population increased, Kilwa's community mosque had to be rebuilt and remodeled several times until finally, when the town was abandoned due to Portuguese attacks in the 16th century, it collapsed. Today, Kilwa is a ruin, a national historical park of the modern nation of Tanzania. Yet other Swahili towns survived the centuries, towns such as Mombasa and Lamu, where the architecture of people's houses and the living Swahili language still echo the greatness of the Swahili civilization in its golden age.

EPILOGUE

When Ibn Battuta left Morocco in 1325 to begin his travels around the Muslim world, he hadn't planned to become an expert on geography or history or local customs. But more than a quarter of a century later, after many years on the road traveling to lands as far away as China, he dictated an account of everything that had happened on his journeys. He wrote of hardships in strange lands, meetings with kings and sultans, unfamiliar foods such as African milk-and-chicken stews and spicy Indian curries—and today his writings are the basis for much of what we know about life in the Middle East, Africa, and Spain in earlier centuries.

In his travels through Africa, Ibn Battuta might have carried a clay canteen shaped like this one, which is made of silver and brass.

In the 700 years between Muhammad's death and Ibn Battuta's travels, Islam, the religion Muhammad had founded, had spread through conquest and trade through much of the world as it was known in the 14th century, from Spain to China. As Ibn Battuta discovered, throughout this vast territory millions of ordinary people as well as kings looked to the collections of God's messages to Muhammad for comfort and guidance. The great 14th-century traveler was able to visit dozens of great Islamic lands because Islam itself connected people across this wide expanse. Although customs and languages differed greatly, Muslims everywhere read many of the same books, observed the same basic religious duties, and understood at least a little Arabic.

Although most of the Africans Ibn Battuta met were Muslims like himself, they had discovered ways of maintaining some of their old ways while being good Muslims. Islam taught that there was only one God, Allah, and one law, God's holy law. Yet African Muslims continued to supplement Islam with ancient religious practices, such as praying to spirits of their dead family members, and to follow old laws that gave greater rights and freedoms to women than Islamic law sometimes allowed. Moreover, since Africans were not Arabs, African Islamic cultures continued to prefer African ways over Arab ways.

Ibn Battuta was a rare sort of traveler because he recorded his impressions, but he was not the only Muslim who journeyed from continent to continent. Three things linked the Middle East and Africa: religion, trade, and travel. All Muslims were required to visit Mecca, the Arab city where Muhammad had been born. So religion provided a basis for the reach of Islamic civilization across many nations. Muslims from Asia, Africa, and even Europe came together in Islam's holiest city by the hundreds of thousands every year and returned to their homes a little more knowledgeable about other lands, other cultures, and even other languages. Trade also led to the weaving of an immense web of routes by which goods and people moved. By the time of Ibn Battuta, this web stretched over most of the known world. In addition, Muslim trade and travel fostered the gathering of an extensive store of knowledge about geography. While Ibn Battuta was perhaps the greatest Muslim traveler, there were dozens of others who traveled for trade, or just for the sake of knowledge, and who wrote about it; still others passed stories down through oral traditions that have survived through centuries and generations. Many of their names and accounts survive in modern libraries. As long as people are curious about the world around them, their history will go on.

GLOSSARY

Abbasids (ab-BAH-sidz) Family of caliphs who ruled the Islamic Empire from 750 to 1258

Alafin (a-LA-fin) Kings of West African forest kingdom of Oyo

Allah (al-LAAH) "God" in Arabic

Almoravids (al-mo-RA-vids) Group of 11th-century Muslims who tried to reform Berber and West African religious observance, and who conquered most of North and West Africa, as well as Spain

Andalusian (an-da-LOO-see-an) Descriptive term for Muslim Spain, taken from Al-Andalus

Arabic (AIR-a-bic) Native language of Arabs

Bantu (BAN-too) African peoples mostly south of the Equator, including Swahili, Shona, and Zulu, who belong to the same language group

Bedouin (BEH-doo-in) Nomadic pastoralist people who live in Arabian desert and commonly herd goats, sheep, camels, mules, and horses and live in tents

Berbers North Africans

Bini (BEE-nee) People of Kingdom of Benin

Byzantine (BIZZ-an-teen) Eastern Roman Empire with capital at Constantinople; Muslims' primary rival for centuries

caliphs (kah-LEEFS) Muslim rulers after Muhammad died

clan Group of families who share a common ancestor

devshirme (dehv-sheer-MEH) Ottoman sultans' system for recruiting non-Muslim boys to train as personal servants and soldiers, from the Turkish word meaning "harvest"

Five Pillars of Islam Basic beliefs and practices followed by all Muslims, including statement of belief, prayer, fasting, pilgrimage, and giving alms to Muslim poor

ghazis (GAH-zees) Soldiers who fought against non-Muslims through jihad, or holy war

griots (GREE-oh) Royal poet-historians of Mali who memorize and recite deeds of king's ancestors

hadiths (hah-DEETHS) Reports of Muhammad's words and deeds and of other early Muslims

harem (HAIR-rum) Private rooms of a Muslim's home or palace where women live

hijra Muhammad's flight to Medina in 622

House of Wisdom Translation bureau founded by Abbasid caliphs in Baghdad; later, a research institute for Muslims of Abbasid period

imam (ih-MOM) Shiite term for rightful spiritual leader of entire Islamic community; Shiites believe he is a direct descendant of Ali

Islam (is-LAAM) Monotheistic religion founded by Muhammad

Janissaries (JAN-ih-sayr-eez) Special servants of the Ottoman sultans, chosen from Christian families

jihad (jee-HAAD) Arabic word for a holy war fought against unbelievers

jizya (JIZZ-ya) Special tax that Muslims required non-Muslims to pay in return for religious freedom and protection

Ka'ba (KAH-bah) Muslim shrine in Mecca, meaning "cube"; considered to be center of Muslim world

Kharijites (KAH-rih-jites) Arabic for "those who exit," referring to a branch of Islam that did not support caliphs after Ali as leaders of Muslim community

kraals (CRAWLS) Corrals used to contain herds of cattle

Mandinke (man-DING-kay) People who live in Sahel and on grassland savannah of West Africa; people of Kingdom of Mali

Mansa (MAHN-sa) Family of kings of Kingdom of Mali

mawalis (ma-WAH-lees) Term applied to non-Arabs who converted to Islam during years of Umayyad caliphs

Muslims (MUS-lims) Followers of Islamic religion, who believe in God (Allah) and Muhammad

Mutazilites (moo-TA-zi-lites) Philosophers who wanted to make Islamic beliefs abide by rules of logic

oasis (o-WAY-sis) Fertile place in desert that has a source of water, such as natural springs and wells

Oba (AW-ba) Title of kings of Benin

Oni (OO-nee) Title of kings of Ifé

oral tradition Stories, poems, and songs composed and recited entirely from memory and by word of mouth in order to preserve a past record among people who do not have a written language

Oyo (aw-yaw) Forest kingdom of Yoruba people

Quran (ku-RAAN) God's messages to Muhammad collected into one book in 655

Quraysh (KOO-resh) Arab tribe of Mecca into which Muhammad was born

rain forest Area that gets a lot of rain, has a wet and humid climate, and is covered with dense forest

Ramadan (ra-ma-DHAN) Muslim month of fasting

ribat (rih-BAHT) Monastery-like place where Muslims can go to study Islamic religious subjects

rihla (RIH-la) Arabic word for a long journey to see the world

Sahel (sa-HEL) Narrow strip of Africa between Sahara Desert and savannah grasslands

Sanhaja (san-HA-ja) Large association of Berber tribes of western Sahara who control most of its caravan trade

savannah (sah-VA-nah) Flat plain on which mostly grasses grow, and a few trees; it has two rainy seasons and two dry seasons a year

Sassanid (SAAS-sa-nid) Name of last dynasty of kings (224–651) to rule Persian Empire before Muslims conquered it

Seljuk (SEL-juck) Family of Turkish rulers, or sultans, who took over control of Baghdad and Abbasid caliphate in late 900s and remained powerful until defeated by 13th-century Mongols

Sharia (shah-REE-uh) Islamic law as established in Quran and Sunna

shaykh (SHAKE) Tribal leader among Arab Bedouins; also a respectful form of address for a religious leader

Shiite (SHEE-ite) Branch of Muslims who believe that Muhammad chose his son-in-law Ali and his descendants to lead all Muslims

Soninke (so-NING-kay) West African people of Kingdom of Ghana

Sosso (SOS-so) Soninke people who became powerful after Ghana Empire fell and before Mali Empire rose to power

steppe (STEP) Geographic term for a large plain that has no trees

Sufi (SOO-fee) Muslim mystic, a follower of popular Islam that emphasizes spontaneous and emotional experiences of God

Sunna (SUH-nuh) "The trodden path" in Arabic; Islamic customs and beliefs based on living example provided by Muhammad

Sunnis (SOO-nees) Main body of believers in Islam

Topkapi (top-KA-puh) **Palace** Great palace of Ottoman sultans in Istanbul

tribe Collection of several clans

Tuareg (TWA-reg) Large Berber tribe of central Sudan in West Africa who controlled caravan trade of that region for many centuries

ulama (oo-la-MAH) Muslim religious scholars, doctors of religious law

Umayyad Dynasty of caliphs from 661 to 750

Umma Muslim term for entire worldwide community of Muslims

Yoruba (yo-roo-BAH) People living in rain forest in what is now Nigeria

zakat (zuh-KAT) Charitable tax required of Muslims

zejel (ZEH-hel) Type of poetry that was developed in Andalusian Spain

TIMELINE

570
Axum besieges Mecca; Muhammad is born in Mecca, a city in west-central Arabia

610
Muhammad reportedly receives his first message from God

622
Muhammad and followers flee from Mecca to Medina

627
Meccans' last attempt to destroy Muslims ends in failure at Battle of Ditch

630
Muhammad performs first pilgrimage to Mecca

632
Muhammad dies; selection of first caliph, Abu Bakr, takes place

632–634
Muslims conquer Arabia

634
Selection of second caliph, Umar; Muslim conquests begin outside of Arabia

around 640–720
Muslims take over Maghrib, their name for northwest Africa

653
Caliph Uthman orders that Quran be written down

656–661
Civil war erupts between Ali and Muawiya

661–750
Umayyad caliphs reign in Damascus

680
Civil war erupts between Umayyads and followers of Husayn, son of Ali; Husayn is murdered at Karbala

700s–800s
Muslim traders arrive in western and central Sudan

700s–1000s
Gao, Jenne, and Kumbi Saleh are early and important centers of caravan trade of western Sudan

711–1498
Muslims invade and occupy Spain, which they call Al-Andalus

750
Abbasid caliphate is formally established

750–900
First city-states are founded on East African coast

762–763
Caliph al-Mansur founds Baghdad, capital city of great Abbasid caliphs

786–809
Harun al-Rashid reigns in Baghdad

800s–900s
First Sudanese convert to Islam

809–833
Al-Ma'mun reigns

900s–1000s
Gao, city southeast of great bend of Niger River, is major trade center of Ghana at its height

900s–1200s
East Africans trade heavily with Persian Gulf

1036 and 1076
Almoravids wage jihad to unify Berbers of western Sudan and impose stricter forms of Islam

around 1055
Seljuk Turks establish sultanate in Baghdad

around 1060–1123
Omar Khayyám lives

1071
Seljuk Turks win Battle of Manzikert and invade Anatolia

1100 to 1425
Great Zimbabwe, east-central African kingdom, flourishes

1100s–1500s
Yoruba kingdom of Ifé flourishes in West Africa's rain forest

around 1200s–1400s
Swahili cities fight for control of Sofala

1200s–1400s
African kingdom of Great Zimbabwe is at its height

1235
Sundiata becomes first king of Mali Empire

around 1250
Abu'l-Mawahib dynasty is founded at Kilwa, greatest of Swahili city-states

1258
Mongols destroy Baghdad; Osman establishes Ottoman Empire

1300
Kingdom of Benin is founded in West African rain forest

1300s–1400s
Buré is principal source of gold trade of Mali

1300s–1700s
Bitu is important source of gold trade of Jenne

1324–1325
Mansa Musa of Mali makes his pilgrimage to Mecca

1325–1354
Ibn Battuta travels around world during his *rihla*

1326–1359
Orhan reigns in Anatolia

1400s–1500s
Gao is center of Songhay Empire

1400–1450
Great Zimbabwe is abandoned and Kingdom of Mwenemutapa is founded in southern Africa

1400–1591
Mali is in decline; Songhay begins expansion

1400s–1800s
Oyo, a forest kingdom of Yoruba, thrives

1451–1481
Ottoman sultan Mehmed II reigns

1498
Ferdinand and Isabella drive last Muslims out of Spain

1499
Portuguese explorer Vasco da Gama arrives in East Africa and India

1520–1566
Suleyman the Magnificent reigns

1567–1600
Portuguese occupy Mwenemutapa

1591
Songhay Empire falls

FURTHER READING

GENERAL WORKS

[66] Al-Tabari. *The History of al-Tabari.* Translated by I. K. A. Howard. Albany: State University of New York Press, 1990.

Andrea, Alfred J., and James H. Overfield. *The Human Record: Sources of Global History.* Boston: Houghton Mifflin, 2005.

Davidson, Basil, ed. *African Civilization Revisited. From Antiquity to Modern Times.* Trenton, N.J.: Africa World, 1991.

Davis, William Stearns, ed. *Readings in Ancient History: Illustrative Extracts from the Sources.* Boston: Allyn and Bacon, 1912-13.

Garlake, Peter. *The Kingdoms of Africa.* Oxford: Elsevier-Phaidon, 1978.

McNeill, William H., and Marilyn R. Waldman. *The Islamic World.* Chicago: University of Chicago Press, 1973.

[66] Procopius. *History of the Wars.* Translated by H. B. Dewing. Cambridge, Mass.: Harvard University Press, 1914.

ATLASES

[66] Indicopleustes, Cosmas. *The Christian Topography of Cosmas, an Egyptian Monk.* Translated by J. W. McCrindle. London: Hakluyt Society, 1898.

Kasule, Samuel. *The History Atlas of Africa.* New York: Macmillan, 1998.

Morris, Neil, et al. *The Atlas of Islam: People, Daily Life, and Traditions.* New York: Barron's Educational, 2003.

Murray, Jocelyn. *The Cultural Atlas of Africa.* New York: Facts on File, 1998.

BIOGRAPHIES AND AUTOBIOGRAPHIES

Amrouche, Fadhma A. M. *My Life Story: The Autobiography of a Berber Woman.* New Brunswick, N.J.: Rutgers University Press, 1989.

Armstrong, Karen. *Muhammad: A Biography of the Prophet.* San Francisco: HarperSanFrancisco, 1992.

Burns, Kephra, et al. *Mansa Musa: The Lion of Mali.* San Diego: Harcourt Brace, 2001.

Donini, Pier Giovanni. *Arab Travelers and Geographers.* London: Immel, 1991.

[66] ibn Ishaq ibn Yasar, Muhammad. *The Life of Muhammad. A Translation of Ibn Ishaq's Sirat Rasul Allah.* Translated by A. Guillaume. Lahore, Pakistan: Oxford University Press, 1955.

ENCYCLOPEDIAS AND DICTIONARIES

Esposito, John L., ed. *The Islamic World: Past and Present.* 3 vols. New York: Oxford University Press, 2004.

Imperato, Pascal James. *Historical Dictionary of Mali,* 3rd ed. Lanham, Md.: Scarecrow Press, 1996.

Page, Willie F. *Encyclopedia of African History and Culture.* New York: Facts on File, 2001.

ARTS AND SCIENCES

[66] Ibn Battuta. *Travels in Asia and Africa, 1325–1354.* Translated and edited by H. A. R. Gibb. London: Broadway House, 1929.

Beshore, George. *Science in Early Islamic Culture.* New York: Franklin Watts, 1998.

Foster, Edward, trans. *The Turkish Letters of Ogier Ghiselin de Busbecq, Imperial Ambassador at Constantinople, 1554–1562.* Oxford: Clarendon Press, 1927.

Goodman, Lenn Evan, trans. and ed. *Ibn Tufayl's Hayy Ibn Yaqzan.* New York: Twayne, 1972.

Goodwin, Godfrey. *A History of Ottoman Architecture.* Baltimore, Md.: Johns Hopkins University Press, 1971.

Heath, Peter. *Thirsty Sword; Sirat Antar and the Arabic Popular Epic.* Salt Lake City: University of Utah Press, 1996.

Helminski, Kabir, trans. *The Rumi Collection: An Anthology of Translations of Mevlana Jalaluddin Rumi.* Brattleboro, Vt.: Threshold Books, 1998.

Irwin, Robert. *The Alhambra.* Cambridge, Mass.: Harvard University Press, 2004.

Keenan, Brigid. *Damascus: Hidden Treasures of the Old City.* New York: Thames & Hudson, 2000.

Khayyam, Omar. *The Rubaiyat of Omar Khayyam.* Translated by Edward Fitzgerald. Garden City, N.Y.: Doubleday, 1930.

Macaulay, David. *Mosque.* Boston: Houghton Mifflin, 2003.

Marzolph, Ulrich, and Richard van Leeuwen. *The Arabian Nights Encyclopedia.* Santa Barbara, Calif.: ABC-CLIO, 2004.

Mathers, Powys, trans. *The Book of the Thousand Nights and One Night.* Boston: Routledge & Kegan Paul, 1986.

Saudi Aramco World. Bimonthly magazine. Houston, Tex.: Aramco Services.

Wilkinson, Philip, and Batul Salazar. *Eyewitness Islam.* New York: Dorling Kindersley, 2002.

FOREST KINGDOMS

Collins, Robert O. *West African History.* New York: Markus Wiener, 1990.

Elliot, Kit. *Benin: An African Kingdom and Culture.* Minneapolis: Lerner, 1979.

Isichei, Elizabeth. *History of Nigeria.* New York: Longman, 1983.

Koslow, Phillip. *Yorubaland: The Flowering of Genius.* New York: Chelsea House, 1996.

Levtzion, Nehemia, ed., and J. F. P. Hopkins, trans. *Corpus of Early Arabic Sources for West African History.* New York: Cambridge University Press, 1981.

Mann, Kenny. *Oyo, Benin, Ashanti: The Guinea Coast.* Parsippany, N.J.: Dillon Press, 1996.

Millar, Heather. *The Kingdom of Benin in West Africa.* Tarrytown, N.Y.: Benchmark Books, 1996.

GREAT ZIMBABWE AND THE SHONA

Garlake, Peter. *Life at Great Zimbabwe.* Gweru, Zimbabwe: Mambo Press, 1983.

Phillipson, D. W. *The Later Prehistory of Eastern and Southern Africa.* London: Heinemann Educational Books, 1977.

MUHAMMAD AND EARLY ISLAM

Armstrong, Karen. *Muhammad: A Biography of the Prophet.* San Francisco: HarperSanFrancisco, 1993.

Cragg, Kenneth, ed. and trans. *Readings from the Qur'an.* London: Collins Liturgical Publications, 1988.

Lewis, Bernard. *The Arabs in History.* New York: Oxford University Press, 1993.

Swisher, Clarice. *The Spread of Islam.* San Diego, Calif.: Greenhaven Press, 1998.

NORTH AFRICA AND SPAIN

Al-Andalus: A Compilation from Saudi Aramco World. Houston, Tex.: Aramco Services, 2004.

Boville, Edward W. *The Golden Trade of the Moors: West African Kingdoms in the Fourteenth Century.* New York: Markus Wiener, 2001.

Ecker, Heather. *Caliphs and Kings: The Art and Influence of Islamic Spain.* Seattle: University of Washington Press, 2004.

OTTOMAN EMPIRE

Addison, John. *Suleyman and the Ottoman Empire.* San Diego, Calif.: Greenhaven Press, 1986.

[66] Ali, Mustafa. *Counsel for Sultans of 1581.* Translated by Andreas Tietze. Vienna: Verlag der Osterreichischen Akademie der Wissenschaften, 1979.

Atil, Esin. *Suleymanname: The Illustrated History of Suleyman the Magnificent.* Washington, D.C.: National Gallery of Art, 1986.

Goodwin, Jason. *Lords of the Horizons: A History of the Ottoman Empire.* New York: Henry Holt, 1999.

Greenblatt, Miriam. *Suleyman the Magnificent and the Ottoman Empire.* New York: Benchmark Books, 2002.

Itzkowitz, Norman. *Ottoman Empire and Islamic Tradition.* Chicago: University of Chicago Press, 1990.

Ruggiero, Adriane. *The Ottoman Empire.* New York: Benchmark Books, 2003.

SUDANIC KINGDOMS

Burns, Khephra, et al. *Mansa Musa: The Lion of Mali.* San Diego, Calif.: Gulliver Books, 2001.

[66] Conrad, David C., ed. and trans. *Sunjata: A West African Epic of the Mande Peoples,* narrated by Djanka Tassey Condé. Indianapolis: Hackett Publishing, 2004.

[66] Hudwick, John O. *Timbuktu and the Songhay Empire: Al-Sadi's Ta'rikh al-Sudan Down to 1613 and Other Contemporary Documents.* Boston: Brill, 1999.

[66] Johnson, John W., trans. *Son-Jara: The Mande Epic.* Bloomington: Indiana University Press, 2004.

———, et al., eds. *Oral Epics from Africa: Vibrant Voices from a Vast Continent.* Bloomington: Indiana University Press, 1997.

Koslow, Phillip J. *Songhay: The Empire Builders.* New York: Chelsea House, 1994.

Mann, Kenny. *Western Sudan: Ghana, Mali, Songhay.* New York: Silver Burdett, 1996.

Masoff, Joy, and Barbara Brown. *Mali: Land of Gold and Glory.* Waccabuc, N.Y.: Five Ponds Press, 2001.

McKissack, Frederick, and Patricia McKissack. *The Royal Kingdoms of Ghana, Mali and Songhay: Life in Medieval Africa.* New York: Henry Holt, 1994.

[66] Niane, Djibril Tamsir. *Sundiata,* Translated by G. D. Pickett. London: Longman, 1965.

Quigley, Mary. *Ancient West African Kingdoms: Ghana, Mali, and Songhai.* London: Heinemann Educational Books, 2002.

THE SWAHILI

[66] Camões, Luís Vas de. *The Lusiads.* Translated by Landeg White. New York: Oxford University Press, 2002.

[66] Freeman-Grenville, G. S. P., ed. *The East African Coast: Select Documents.* New York: Oxford University Press, 1962.

Garlake, Peter. *The Kingdoms of Africa.* Oxford: Phaidon Press, 1978.

Mann, Kenny. *Zenj, Buganda: East Africa.* Parsippany, N.J.: Dillon Press, 1996.

WEBSITES

INDEX

TEXT CREDITS

p.17: Procopius, *History of the Wars,* vol. 1, trans. H. B. Dewing (Cambridge, Mass.: Harvard University Press, 1914; reprint ed., 1953–54), 179–95.

pp.18–19: Cosmas Indicopleustes, *The Christian Topography of Cosmas, an Egyptian Monk,* trans. J. W. McCrindle (London: Hakluyt Society, 1898), 51–53.

p.21: Peter Heath, *The Thirsty Sword: Sirat Antar and the Arabic Popular Epic* (Salt Lake City: University of Utah Press, 1996).

p.25: Lerner, Ralph, and Muhsin Mahdi, eds. *Medieval Political Philosophy: A Sourcebook* (Ithaca, N.Y.: Cornell University Press, 1972), 77.

p.27: Muhammad ibn Ishaq ibn Yasar, *The Life of Muhammad. A Translation of Ibn Ishaq's Sirat Rasul Allah,* trans. A. Guillaume (Lahore, Pakistan: Oxford University Press, 1955), 106.

p.28: Quran, 2:177.

p.29: William H. McNeill and Marilyn R. Waldman, eds., *The Islamic World* (Chicago: University of Chicago Press, 1973), 12.

p.39: Ahmad ibn-Jabir al-Baladhuri, *Kitab Futuh al-Buldha* (The Origins of the Islamic State), trans. P. K. Hitti and F. C. Murgotten, *Studies in History, Economics and Public Law,* LXVIII (New York: Columbia University Press, 1916 and 1924), 207–11.

p.41: Ibn Khaldun, *History of the Berbers* (Paris: Paul Geuthner, 1999).

p.48: Alfred J. Andrea and James H. Overfield, *The Human Record: Sources of Global History,* vol. 1 (Boston: Houghton Mifflin, 2005), 256.

p.51: Ibn Battuta, *Travels in Asia and Africa 1325–1354,* trans. and ed. H. A. R. Gibb (London: Broadway House, 1929), 65–66.

p.52: I. K. A. Howard, trans., *The History of al-Tabari,* vol. XIX (Albany: State University of New York Press, 1990).

p.58: William Stearns Davis, ed., *Readings in Ancient History: Illustrative Extracts from the Sources,* vol. 2 (Boston: Allyn and Bacon, 1912–13), 365–67. (Scanned and modernized by Dr. Jerome S. Arkenberg, Department of History, California State University, Fullerton.)

p.62: Ibn Battuta, *Travels in Asia and Africa 1325–1354,* trans. and ed. H. A. R. Gibb (London: Broadway House, 1929), 100–1.

p.64: Kenneth Cragg, trans., *Readings in the Qur'an* (London: Collins Liturgical Publications, 1988), 292–93.

p.70: Quran, 5:38.

p.72: C. E. Bosworth, trans., *The History of al-Tabari,* vol. XXXII (Albany: State University of New York Press, 1987), 199–200.

p.76: Kabir Helminski, ed. and trans., *The Rumi Collection: An Anthology of Translations of Mevlana Jalaluddin Rumi* (Brattleboro, Vt.: Threshold Books, 1998), 152.

p.79: Lenn Evan Goodman, trans. and ed., *Ibn Tufayl's Hayy Ibn Yaqzan* (New York: Twayne, 1972), 106, 109–10.

pp.84–85: Powys Mathers, trans., *The Book of the Thousand Nights and One Night,* vol. 1 (New York: Routledge, 1986), 29–30.

p.101: Edward Foster, trans., *The Turkish Letters of Ogier Ghiselin de Busbecq, Imperial Ambassador at Constantinople, 1554–1562* (Oxford: Clarendon Press, 1927), 58–59, 65–66.

p.102: Mustafa Ali, *Counsel for Sultans of 1581,* vol. 1, trans. Andreas Tietze (Vienna: Verlag der Osterreichischen Akademie der Wissenschaften, 1979), 39.

p.104: J. F. P. Hopkins, trans., and Nehemiah Levtzion and J. F. P. Hopkins, eds., *Corpus of Early Arabic Sources for West African History* (New York: Cambridge University Press, 1981), 48–49.

p.107: Ibid.

p.109: Ibid., 79–80.

p.110: Ibid., 236.

p.112: Ibid., 48–49.

p.113: Ibid., 236.

p.114: Maurice Delafosse, ed., *Notes Africaines* (Dakar: Institut Français d'Afrique Noire, 1959), cited in Basil Davidson, *African Civilization Revisited: From*

Antiquity to Modern Times (Trenton, N.J.: Africa World Press, 1991), 88–89.

p.117: Robert O. Collins, *Western African History* (New York: Markus Wiener, 1990), 26.

p.119: D. T. Niane, *Sundiata: An Epic of Old Mali* (Essex, England: Longman, 1997), 63.

p.121: Robert O. Collins, *Western African History* (New York: Markus Wiener, 1990), 23.

p.122: Alfred J. Andrea and James H. Overfield, *The Human Record: Sources of Global History,* 5th ed., vol. 1 (Boston and New York: Houghton Mifflin, 2005), 258.

p.132: *Church Missionary Intelligencer* (1854), 58. Quoted in Elizabeth Isichei, *A History of Nigeria* (New York: Longman, 1983), 131.

p.133: Jacob Egharevba, *A Short History of Benin,* 3rd ed. (Ibadan University Press, 1960). From Basil Davidson, *African Civilization Revisited* (Trenton, N.J.: Africa World Press, 1991), 123.

pp. 134–35: Ibid., 121–22.

p.136: http://www.wsu.edu:8080/~wldciv/world_civ_reader/world_civ_reader_2/eden.html.

p.137: Ibid.

p.140: Friedrich W. T. Posselt, trans., *The Idea of God Among South African Tribes.* Quoted in Edwin W. Smith, ed., *African Ideas of God: A Symposium* (London, 1950), 127.

p.147: George M. Theal, *Records of South-Eastern Africa, Collected in Various Libraries and Archive Departments in Europe,* vol. 1 (London, 1898). Reprinted in Robert O. Collins, *Central and South African History* (New York: Markus Wiener, 1990), 62–68.

p.151: João de Barros, *Da Asia,* decade 1, book 8, trans. George M. Theal, *Records of Southeastern Africa,* vol. VI (London, 1900). Quoted in Greville S. P. Freeman-Grenville, *The East African Coast, Select Documents from the First to the Earlier Nineteenth Century* (Oxford: Clarendon Press, 1962), 85–86.

p.152: Ibn Battuta, *Travels in Asia and Africa 1325–1354,* trans. and ed. H. A. R. Gibb (London: Broadway House, 1929), 112–13.

p.155: Greville S. P. Freeman-Grenville, *The East African Coast: Select Documents from the First to the Earlier Nineteenth Century* (Oxford: Clarendon Press, 1962), 123–24.

p.158: Luiz Vaz de Camões, *The Lusiads,* trans. and ed. Landeg White (Oxford: Oxford University Press, 2001), 23.

PICTURE CREDITS

© Art Resource, NY: 40 (© Cameraphoto Arte, Venice), 44 (© Gilles Mermet), 54 (© Reunion des Musees Nationaux), 65, 101 (© Giraudon), 106 (© Aldo Tutino), 127 (© Newark Museum); © Robert Azzi–Woodfin Camp: 15; © Bildarchiv Preussischer Kulturbesitz/Art Resource, NY: 28, 47, 59, 60; Bodleian Library, University of Oxford: 82; www.bridgeman.co.uk: 78 (Egyptian National Library, Cairo, Egypt, Giraudon), 108 (Private Collection, Michael Graham-Stewart), 124 (Bibliotheque Nationale, Paris, France, Archives Charmet), 137 (Nationalmuseet, Copenhagen, Denmark), 140 (Private Collection, Heini Schneebeli); © Bridgeman-Giraudon/Art Resource, NY: 45, 50, 71, 74, 2, 92; By permission of British Library: 75; © Trustees of the Chester Beatty Library, Dublin: 42; © Erich Lessing/Art Resource, NY: 18, 23, 24, 32, 38, 53, 77, 96, 111; Freer Gallery of Art, Smithsonian Institution, Washington, D.C.: cover text (F1929.28), 62 (F1927.3), 66 (F1949.14), 160 (F1941.10); Photo by Brice Hammack: 87; © HIP/Art Resource, NY: 120, 132; UA104, Poster Collection. Hoover Institution Archives: 34; Mamma Haidara Commemorative Library, Timbuktu, in Library of Congress Online Exhibition, "Ancient Manuscripts," 2003: 126; Metropolitan Museum of Art: cover (Purchase, Edith Perry Chapman fund, Rogers, Pfeiffer, Fletcher, and Dodge Funds, Gift of Humanities Fund Inc., by exchange, Mrs. Donald M. Olenslager Gift in memory of her husband, Geert CE Prins Gift, and funds from Various Donors, 1977 (1977.173) Photograph © 1978 MMA), 89 (Rogers Fund, 1955 (55.44) Photograph © 1992 MMA), 95 (Purchase, Harris Brisbane Dick Fund, Joseph Pulitzer Bequest, Louis V. Bell Fund and Fletcher, Pfeiffer, and Rogers Funds, 1990 (1990.61) Photograph © MMA); Minneapolis Institute of Arts, John R. Van Derlip Fund: 131; Lynn Abercrombie/National Geographic Image Collection: 26; © Peter Langer–Associated Media Group www.peterlanger.com: 139, 143, 144; © Pierpont Morgan Library/Art Resource, NY: 68, 110, 152; Saudi Aramco World/PADIA: 80 (Tor Eigeland), 91 (David H. Wells); © Scala/Art Resource, NY: 20, 67, 85; © SEF/Art Resource, NY: 30, 57; © Snark/Art Resource, NY: 61, 76; F. Rigaud/Travel-Images.com: 13; Photo by Jim Steinhart of www.TravelPhotoBase.com: 155; © Vanni/Art Resource, NY: 43, 99, 100; © Victoria & Albert Museum, London/Art Resource, NY: 48, 63; © Werner Forman/Art Resource, NY: 16, 19, 27, 36, 83, 103, 105, 113, 115, 118, 123, 128, 129, 135, 145, 146, 149, 151, 157, 158.

ACKNOWLEDGMENTS

The author would like to thank editor Karen Fein at Oxford University Press for her marvelous job of helping an academic present the fruits of his research to young readers. Nancy Toff and Bonnie Smith also deserve thanks for their helpful comments on each draft of the manuscript. In addition Tara Deal merits credit for her work with the line editing, Harriet Jackson for research in finding suitable, additional quotes, and Elizabeth Pollock and James Cleary for helping with the text preparation.

RANDALL L. POUWELS is professor of African and Islamic history at the University of Central Arkansas. He is the author of *Horn and Crescent: Cultural Change and Traditional Islam on the East African Coast, 800–1900*; co-editor (with Nehemia Levtzion) of *The History of Islam in Africa* and co-author of *World Civilizations*. Pouwels serves on the editorial board of the French historical journal *Afrique et Histoire* (Africa and History) and was a founder and the first president of the African Islamic Studies Association of the African Studies Association. He has done extensive field research in Africa and has received grants from the National Geographic Society, the American Council of Learned Societies, the National Endowment for the Humanities, and the American Philosophical Society.

BONNIE G. SMITH is Board of Governors Professor of History at Rutgers University. She has edited a series for teachers on Women's and Gender History in Global Perspective for the American Historical Association and has served as chair of the test development committee for the Advanced Placement examination in European history. Professor Smith is the author of many books on European, comparative, and women's history, among them *Confessions of a Concierge* and *Imperialism: A History in Documents*. She is co-author of *The Making of the West: Peoples and Cultures*, editor in chief of the forthcoming Oxford encyclopedia on women in world history, and general editor of an Oxford world history series for high school students and general readers.